T0133678

Drupal
Web
Profiles

Drupal Web Profiles

Timi Ogunjobi

CRC Press
Taylor & Francis Group
Boca Raton   London   New York

CRC Press is an imprint of the
Taylor & Francis Group, an **informa** business
AN AUERBACH BOOK

CRC Press
Taylor & Francis Group
6000 Broken Sound Parkway NW, Suite 300
Boca Raton, FL 33487-2742

Printed in the United States of America on acid-free paper
Version Date: 20120611

International Standard Book Number: 978-1-4665-0381-6 (Hardback)

Visit the Taylor & Francis Web site at
http://www.taylorandfrancis.com

and the CRC Press Web site at
http://www.crcpress.com

Contents

Preface

This is a book about how to create effective business web solutions using Drupal. The book provides instructions on the primary aspects of the Drupal framework; from basic installation, configuration and administration to creating new functionality, look and feel through custom modules and themes. It also shows how to rapidly prototype and build powerful web applications using Drupal builds or profiles; which are Drupal distributions that have already been pre-configured with the required modules for the creation of specific types of web applications.

Overview

The first five chapters of the book contain instructions to install, configure and administer a basic site in using either version 6 or 7 of Drupal. The next five chapters introduce Drupal profiles and gives basic information on how to get them set up and working. The last chapter gives advice on how to monitor, analyze and optimize the performance of your Drupal installation.

Chapter 1   Introduction to Drupal

This chapter shows the basic Drupal terminologies and terms of interest to both users and developers. It also shows how to create an installation environment for Drupal and how to carry out the actual installation. The reader is given information on where to get further online resources for working with Drupal.

Chapter 2   Adding, Classifying and Viewing Content

In this chapter, the user learns how to add new content to a Drupal site and how to describe, classify, and organize content on the site by using the *Taxonomy module*. Users will also learn how to create an effective taxonomy structure, as well as how to port an existing static HTML site into the Drupal framework.

Chapter 3   Administering Drupal

This chapter gives an overview of the administrative tools available on a Drupal site. It briefly explains the administrative features of Drupal and how to use these features to ensure your site performs optimally. These features cover security and performance issues that a live site will contend with on a daily basis along with hints on how to prevent them. The user will also learn how to backup a Drupal site and how to migrate it from one server to another.

Chapter 4   Drupal Themes

This chapter demonstrates how the theme system functions. The various components of a Drupal theme are explained here along with how to determine the required/optional theme components. The chapter shows how to proceed with the construction of a new theme from scratch, using the default PHPTemplate theme engine. This chapter examines the typical structure of the component theme files and gives advice on how to create similar structures for a custom theme.

Chapter 5   Drupal Modules

In this chapter, the user learns the structure of a Drupal module, how to create a Drupal module, and where to find resources to develop a custom Drupal module. The user will also learn how to test and troubleshoot the resulting module if necessary.

Chapter 6   Creating a Community Site with Drupal Commons

This chapter shows how to install and perform the basic configuration of a community site built with the Acquia Commons development framework. It demonstrates the various stages of the installation process and identifies available features.

Chapter 7   Building a Conference Site with COD

This chapter shows how to create a conference site with the Drupal COD distribution. It shows how to install the software and takes the user through the basic configuration. The chapter identifies the salient features of an installed COD site and shows how to administer the features to create a functional and effective conference management framework.

Chapter8   Creating a News Publishing Site with OpenPublish

This chapter shows how to create a news publishing site with the Drupal OpenPublish distribution. It shows how to install the software and takes the user through the basic configuration. The chapter identifies the important features of an installed OpenPublish site and shows how to administer the site to create a functional and effective news publishing framework.

Chapter 9   Creating an Intranet with Open Atrium

An intranet facilitates communication between people or work groups to improve the knowledge base of an organization's employees. It typically consists of an internal email system, a message board service, internal web sites, a database, and a document management system. This chapter shows how to create an intranet site with the Drupal Open Atrium distribution. It shows how to install the software and takes the user through the basic configuration. The chapter identifies the important features of the installed Open Atrium site and shows how to administer them to create a functional and effective intranet framework.

Chapter 10   Creating an online Learning Management System with ELMS

This chapter describes how to create an online learning management system with the e-Learning Management System (ELMS). It shows how to install the software and takes the user through the basic configuration. The chapter identifies the important features of an ELMS site and takes the reader through the basics of how to create and administer the features of a functional ELMS framework.

Chapter 11   Analyzing, Monitoring and Optimizing

The purpose of this chapter is to show how to improve the performance of a Drupal website for the benefit of users as well as other stakeholders. This can be effected by following good practice suggestions that help to effectively monitor, optimize and analyze the performance of a live site. The chapter also provides suggestions for required and optional core features. It advises on where to get additional tools for performance enhancement, primarily by means of contributed modules as well as third party monitoring, optimization and analysis services.

Who is this book for?

The typical user of Drupal Website Profiles will be an IT manager or staff who will be seeking to develop complex web based applications without having an outside developer. The general aim of Drupal Website Profiles is to assist the user to achieve maximum productivity within a short time frame through prototyping preconfigured distribution profiles.

Drupal Website Profiles is written for users with average web design skills. While the contents of this book may greatly assist the user to rapidly develop useful business application with Drupal, it must be emphasized that this book does not endorse the creation of web development of live web applications from profiles primarily because of possible issues of performance. The user is reminded that current Drupal good practices for development and deployment are always recommended.

Acknowledgements

- Many thanks to my entire family who have been a great source of emotional support even though they are so far away
- Many thanks to my agents Carole Jelen McClendon and Zach Romano of Waterside Productions
- Many thanks to my publisher CRC
- Finally thanks to Derryfield Publishing Services for their production work

About the author

Timi Ogunjobi is a software developer, technical author and open source evangelist. Timi has been developing web applications using a variety of frameworks for nearly a decade and has written on a broad range of topics for more than twenty years.

Timi balances his time between programming, reviewing, writing, and contributing to interesting community projects especially those relating to wildlife conservation. When he isn't working, he enjoys playing jazz guitar and getting involved in outdoor activities—principally cricket, golf and swimming.

Timi is the Chief Executive Officer of Xceedia Limited (www.xceedia.co.uk), a software development and training company. Timi has written two other books on Drupal that are currently in print (*Drupal 6 Site Blueprints* and *Drupal 6 Site Blueprints: Lite*). He has also published several fiction and non-fiction books, and has been featured in several anthologies. One of his fiction books has been nominated for the Commonwealth Book Prize.

Chapter 1

Introduction to Drupal

This introductory chapter is to get the reader acquainted with Drupal, its main terminologies and features, as well as how to get a new Drupal site up and running very quickly. It shows various means of acquiring scripts, and how to install Drupal on different computing platforms. It also gives some information about how to get more help and assistance in upgrading your Drupal skills. Following are the highlights:

- What Drupal is and how it is being used?
- What version of Drupal to use
- The basic concepts and terminologies of Drupal
- How to install Drupal
- Where to find additional learning resources for Drupal

1.1   What is Drupal?

Drupal is a free software package that enables users to publish, manage, and organize their content on a web site. It is a web application framework, blogging engine, content management system and framework, originally developed as a bulletin board system by Dries Buytaert, and is today used by many high-traffic web sites and has especially been popular for building online communities. Drupal comes from the Dutch word *"druppel"* which means *"drop"*, as in, *"a drop of water"* (Figure 1.1).

Figure 1.1   Drupal logo

1.2   Who is using Drupal?

Drupal is used for many different web applications, and by many of the top ranking companies all over the world. As a web development tool, Drupal has some basic built-in functionality, which if combined with the scores of free contributed modules, may be used to create quite powerful web applications.

- **Community portal sites.** In a typical community portal, people share content such as images, video, audio and stories with other users.
- **News publishing.** These days it is becoming common for newspapers and magazines to enable online editions to increase their reach, readership and revenue potential. Drupal supplies the advantage of simplicity of use and upgradeability of functionality. Therefore, Drupal is quickly becoming the most popular tool for newspapers and other news organizations to publish their content online.
- **Aficionado sites.** This is a type of web site used by groups of people to share their expertise and enthusiasm for a topic. Typical examples include web sites for discussing automobiles or motor bikes.
- **Corporate web sites.** Since it is web based and has a flexible permissions system, Drupal works well for company intranets. With Drupal, it is very easy to allocate roles and permissions for publishing and accessing content. Key staff no longer has to publish new projects.
- **Resource directories.** Drupal enables registered users to suggest new resources for editors to screen, approve add those resources. Directories are typically used to aggregate similar information.
- **International sites.** The localization features within Drupal enable developers to create sites implemented in a wide range of languages.
- **Education.** Several educational institutions use Drupal. It enables the creation of online learning communities as a supplement to the brick wall classroom.
- **Art, music and multimedia.** As a development framework for community art sites, Drupal provides the means to create multimedia rich websites where users may share, discuss, distribute and rate their work with friends and colleagues.

- **Social networking sites.** Drupal has the features required to build expandable social networking web sites. The modules that enable this are available, adaptable, and free. Many companies presently run their web sites using Drupal (Figure 1.2).

Figure 1.2   Websites using Drupal

1.3   How is Drupal different from other content management systems?

Actually, Drupal may not quite accurately be described as a content management system, but rather a content management framework. A system gives the impression of a rigid, clunky structure, while a framework can be viewed as efficient, extendable, and stable, and this is the basic difference. Drupal is adaptable for any type of dynamic site, and the general view is that any web project that can be conceived, can be built in Drupal.

1.4   How much do you need to know to use Drupal?

Drupal is written in the PHP Hypertext Processor (PHP) language—a high-level programming language used for developing web-based applications. If you need to take greatest advantage of the powerful features of Drupal, it might be worthwhile to learn a bit about PHP and either MySQL or PostgreSQL, which are two of the relational databases used with

Drupal. Having said this, there are thousands of Drupal users who cannot write a line of code.

Drupal has been criticized in the past about its usability. Indeed, new users may find some aspects of Drupal's administration interface confusing and intimidating. It is quite possible to master many competing content management systems in a few days, but it could take you considerably longer to achieve the same level of proficiency using Drupal. The administrative interface of Drupal have been regarded as rather cryptic. This is a problem, which successive versions have strived to solve. Drupal nevertheless offers a sophisticated programming interface for developers. No programming skills are required for basic Drupal web site installation and administration.

The steep initial learning can be daunting but once it is learned you can manipulate Drupal in almost any way you want to.

1.5   What do you need to run Drupal?

Any computing platform that supports the following, will run Drupal:

- Web server able to run PHP (version 4.3.5 or above), as well as Apache, IIS, Lighttpd, and nginx
- MySQL or PostgreSQL database, to store settings and content.

1.6   What version of Drupal should you use?

Drupal comes in several versions and releases, corresponding to the current state of development and updates. Drupal 7.x or Drupal 6.x are the main versions currently used and recommended for download and adoption. In description, 7.5 means, Drupal version 7, release 5. Both version6.x and 7.x are presently supported.

Modules are regarded as quite critical for determining what version of Drupal to use—considering that a module written for one version will not work with another version. At the time of writing this book, if you are new to Drupal and decide to build a site using Drupal 7.x, you will probably find that a lot of the modules available to download are only for version 6.x, and very few or fewer for version 7.x. So one question you may be asking is which of the two main versions to choose

1.6.1   Drupal 6.x or Drupal 7.x

On the matter of selecting what version of Drupal to use, some people think that it really boils down to the functionality you will wish to achieve on an immediate basis. Many modules to extend the functionality of your web project presently exist in Drupal Version 6.x, however an infinite amount of modules cannot actually be used because each module takes up memory and other resources. Most web sites will probably only be able to use 20 to 30 modules. So the questions that ought really to be asked should be:

- Which 20-30 features are most desirable?
- Which of those features are provided in Drupal 6.x and with no module released for Drupal 7.x?

1.6.1.1   Must have or nice to have

If the Drupal 6.x modules that attract you are just "nice to have" and nonessential to your application, it seems quite easy to say go with Drupal 7.x. However, early versions do have great merit, primarily because they and the modules which they employ have been tested. Before deciding to use a module it might be wise to check its history—the activity and dates of its issues queue, and its popularity; unless you can support the upgrade yourself.

Looking down the road, several solid modules for Drupal 5.x were never ported to Drupal 6.x, and some of the Drupal 6.x modules have partially had their functionality absorbed into the core modules of Drupal 7.x.

1.6.1.2   Beware of obsolescence

It is generally advised that if it is possible for you to build your site using the present stable modules and Drupal 6.x, go with that solution if you can live with the consequences. As explained previously, there is the possibility that a site built using outdated versions may not be upgradeable in the future with modules being produced for newer versions. So if an upgrade is seriously needed you may need to code again from scratch.

Often you may find for example that modules, which have been newly written for Drupal 7.x, are no longer upgraded to a later version of Drupal merely because the developer has lost interest, thus leaving you with an unsupported and unusable module when you upgrade Drupal in the future.

1.6.1.3   Security concerns

Modules present security concerns for the mere reason that they are contributed by coders from all over the world and do not undergo any great quality control process. So when you use a new module that has not been tested over time, as well as when you use an older version for which there is no more support, you expose your web site to security breaches.

Unfortunately, you can do little about this because the answer always depends on the module developers, *their* need for the module, and on the user base of contributors to the module. Even until this day, new modules and themes are still being developed for Drupal 5.x which is presently the most popular version.

Thus, the challenges which many will face will be whether to use Drupal 6.x and have your be site less secure, use Drupal 7.x with some of the modules still in beta, or just hope and pray that module developers concentrate on Drupal 7.x and base your development plans on that.

1.6.1.4   Compare release notes

Another important factor in making a choice is to find out what feature you miss by not using other Drupal versions. Many website owners are still happily using Drupal version 5.x, and if you can live with whatever functionality this version offers, you may need to worry less about later versions. However, it is best practice to use the releases and version that are up to date.

1.6.2   What is new in Drupal 7.x

New users of Drupal and who have been tutored with Drupal 7.x might get confused when suddenly presented with the administrator's panel for Drupal 6.x. A lot has changed in this new release. Look at the following excerpts from the release notes for Drupal 7.x:

- UI enhancements to make common tasks easy for 80% of users, default settings smart, privileges the content creator, and simplifies administration.
- Enhanced image handling (resize, crop, etc.)
- A built-in, automated test environment featuring a continuous integration test suite running against every patch for long-term stability of the project

- A version upgrade manager for migration from Drupal 6.x to Drupal 7.x
- Performance and scalability improvements that deliver web content faster via advanced caching, Content Delivery Networks (CDN), and master-slave replication
- Custom fields in core, native data item fields for any content type, including users, taxonomy, and other entities, plus support for translations
- A database abstraction layer, which enables the use of many databases, including Microsoft SQL Server, Oracle, PostgreSQL, MySQL, or SQLite, Maria DB and MongoDB.

1.6.3   What version of Drupal is used in this book?

The main tutorials in this book are conducted in Drupal 7.x which is the latest version. However, many of the hands-on projects in the book feature construction of web applications from publicly available *profiles* which, at the time of this writing, are only available in Drupal 6.x. Therefore, for the web profiles portion of the book, Drupal 6.x will be used as the basis for some of the tutorials.

For both versions, the main difference is actually in the administrative interface because the user interface remains largely unchanged. Once the administrator becomes sufficiently familiar with the terms and features used for one version, it should be fairly easy to see how these are applied to other versions.

1.7   The architecture of Drupal

Drupal is written in PHP and stores data in a relational database such as MySQL. Figure 1.3 illustrates a simplified stack diagram of Drupal.

The *Drupal core* contains a set of files consisting of bootstrapping code and frequently used libraries. The libraries provide the means for the modules to interact, and also facilitate database management and connectivity. Additionally, the libraries enable other features such as internationalization, Unicode support as well as mail and image library abstraction.

1.7.1   Basic concept and features

New Drupal users need to learn some basic terminologies, primarily the description of features and functionality.

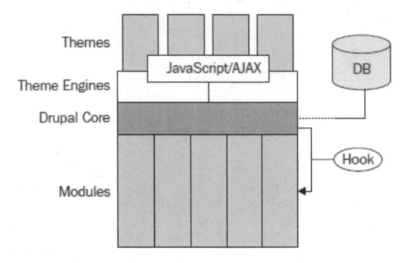

Figure 1.3   The Drupal schema

1.7.2   Node

A *node* in Drupal is the generic term that describes a piece of content on a web site. The node is the most basic description of content on a Drupal site.

Each node on the site will belong to a *content type*. It will also have the following characteristics: A node ID, a title, a creation date, an author, and some other properties. An *author* is a user on the site who has posted content. The *body* of the content may be ignored or omitted for certain *content types*. Figure 1.4 illustrates how nodes are typically listed in the Drupal database:

	nid The primary identifier for a node.	vid The current mod_node_revision.vid version identifier.	type The mod_node_type.type of this node.	language The mod_languages.language of this node.	title The title of this node, always treated as non-markup plain text.	uid The mod_users.uid that owns this node; initially, this is the user that created it.	status Boolean indicating whether the node is published (visible to non-administrators).	created The Unix timestamp when the node was created.
□ ✎ ✕	1	1	page	und	About this site	1	1	1316545400
□ ✎ ✕	2	2	page	und	Contact site administrator	1	1	1316713369
□ ✎ ✕	3	3	page	und	Contact site administrator	1	1	1316713394
⬆ Check All / Uncheck All With selected: ✎ ✕ ▤								

Figure 1.4   The Drupal node table

1.7.3   How nodes work

When you view a Drupal page, the address bar of your browser will probably show something like http://www.mysite.com/node/19828. By this Drupal is indicating "Load all pertinent information for node 19828, including relations, such as comments, users etc., which may be shown". This is called a database query.

Most queries in Drupal are hard coded in modules. Drupal modules perform a lot of operation on the data. For instance, when you open a page, which you have written yourself you see a *view/edit* tab at the top of the page. This tab is not shown on pages you have not written. This is an automated behavior defined by the user privilege settings.

1.7.4   Database

Drupal stores information in a database; each type of information has its own *database table*. For instance, the basic information about the nodes of your site is stored in the node table. Comments, users, roles, permissions, and other settings are also stored in database tables.

1.7.5   Tables

The Drupal data is stored in several dozen tables. Apart from the ones used for the nodes, users and authors also have their own tables. Therefore, nodes have relationships, and those relationships can easily be found by querying

	Table ▾	Action						Records 1	Type	Collatic
☐	mod_actions						✕	12	InnoDB	utf8_general
☐	mod_authmap						✕	0	InnoDB	utf8_general
☐	mod_batch						✕	0	InnoDB	utf8_general
☐	mod_block						✕	30	InnoDB	utf8_general
☐	mod_blocked_ips						✕	0	InnoDB	utf8_general
☐	mod_block_custom						✕	0	InnoDB	utf8_general
☐	mod_block_node_type						✕	0	InnoDB	utf8_general
☐	mod_block_role						✕	0	InnoDB	utf8_general

Figure 1.5   Drupal database table

the tables. Each node can have an unlimited number of comments. However, comments are not nodes and are stored in a separate table. Figure 1.5 is a snapshot of a section of a typical Drupal table.

1.7.6   Taxonomy

Drupalís systemfor classifying content, is known as *taxonomy* and it is implemented in the core *taxonomy* module. Drupal enables users define their own *vocabularies* (groups of taxonomy terms), and add terms to each vocabulary. Vocabularies can be flat or hierarchical, and can allow single or multiple selections. *Free tagging*, is also permitted, meaning that when creating or editing content, users can add new terms on the fly. Each vocabulary can then be attached to one or more content types. In this fashion, nodes can be grouped into categories, tagged, or classified in any way the site administrator chooses.

1.7.7   Module

A module is software code that is used to extend Drupal features and/or functionality. There are two main classes of modules; *core* and *contributed*. Core modules are included in the main distribution of Drupal, and can be activated within Drupal without installing additional software. Some of the core modules in Drupal 7.x started their journey as contributed modules.

Contributed modules can be downloaded from the modules section of the Drupal web site (www.drupal.org). It is not too difficult to create your own modules; but this requires a thorough understanding of Drupal, PHP programming, and the Drupal *module* API.

1.7.8   User, Permission, Role

Every visitor to a Drupal site, (Drupal account holders, and anonymous visitors) is considered a *user* in Drupal. A numeric user ID defines each user. Non-anonymous users also have a user name and an email address. The first user account created when Drupal is installed has a user ID of one (1) and full administrative privileges on the site. Anonymous users have a user ID of zero (0).

All users on the site can be assigned permissions by using the *roles functionality*. To do this, you first need to create roles, which you might for example call ìontent editorî or ìemberî. After doing this, you assign *permissions* to that role. This tells Drupal what the role can and cannot do on the site. Finally, users on the site can be assigned to these role(s). Users will only be permitted to perform actions on the basis of the role(s) they have been assigned to.mc

Drupal permissions are quite flexible and permissions can be assigned for any task and to any role. Some roles such as *anonymous user* (a user who is not logged in) and *authenticated user* (a user who is logged in, with no special role assignments) are default roles, but their permissions can be equally changed.

1.7.9   Comment

A comment is typically a small piece of content submitted by a user in response to a particular node. A comment is not a node and does not get stored in the node table of the database. For example, every subsequent discussion attached to a forum topic posted as a node is a comment. Comments can be implemented by merely enabling the core *comment* module.

1.7.10   Path

The part of the URL after the base site address, is known as the *path*. This path will determine what modules are called to display the page. For example for a page with the URL, http://www.mysite.com/node/19828, the path is *node/19828*.

1.7.11   Theme

The graphical look, layout, and colors of the site is controlled by the theme which typically consists of several PHP files that define the HTML output of the site's pages, as well as one or more CSS files which define the layout, fonts, colors, and other styles.

1.7.12   Regions and blocks

Drupal site pages are laid out in *regions*. Default regions include the header, footer, sidebars, and main content section. It is customary for Drupal themes to define additional regions. *Blocks* are information are displayed within each region of the site. Blocks can be used to render such content as *menus* for site navigation, the output from modules, as well as other static and dynamic chunks of information which have been created by permitted users (e.g., a list of upcoming events). Figure 1.6 illustrates how the regions and blocks are laid out in a typical Drupal theme.

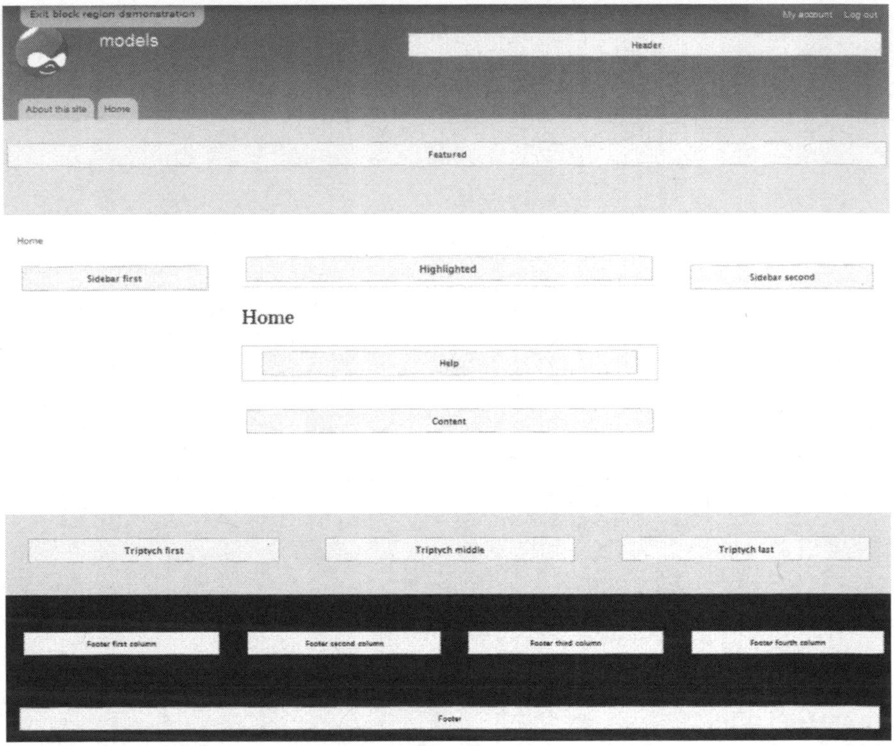

Figure 1.6   Typical block regions

1.7.13 Menu

There are three default menu types in Drupal and they are : *primary links*, *secondary links*, and *navigation*. These links may be built by site administrators, and are automatically displayed in the page header of many themes if their block are enabled to display them. Navigation links   contain the administration menus, as well as links supplied by modules on the site. Additionally to this, administrators and permitted users can also create custom menus, which will be made available in the blocks administration page, for display on the site.

There are several ways to customize menus. The items can be reordered either by setting their *weight* or simply dragging them into place. The items may also be renamed, the link title and paths altered, and the item may even be moved into a different menu by simply editing the *parent* property of the item.

Custom menu items may be added to a menu, through providing the path to a linked content. In all cases, a menu item is visible to a user if they have the permission to view the page it links to. For example, the administrative menu items are visible only to users who have administrator privileges.

1.7.14   Menus and blocks

All menus are displayed in blocks but before they can be visible, the menu module must be enabled. Navigation is the default menu, but as aforementioned, more menus can be created and placed in block regions as desired. A menu must be activated in the blocks settings, where you determine and the location you want the menu menus to be displayed. After this items can be moved to this menu by changing the item's parent property. Custom blocks may also be created and can contain plain text, HTML code, and PHP code.

1.7.15   Themes and modules

After a basic web site has been created, there may be the desire for it to do more than the ordinary and to have the sort of power and look that is often seen on professional web sites. This is where the extra themes and modules come into play. Themes are the elements that make the web site good to look at, and easily navigable. They determine how each page looks. Drupal comes with some basic themes, which can be modified without much difficulty.

Modules on the other hand are the back-end engine of the site and contain the programming which makes a site do extraordinary things. However, there are dozens of modules available, and the real work may be how to find the ones that suit the specific need, and to make them work together.

1.7.16   Content types

Interactive websites typically contain many types of content, such as news, information, polls, blog posts, etc. A content item in Drupal is referred to as a *node*, and each node normally belongs to a single *content type* which characterizes all nodes, and determines their default settings, such as whether the node is to be automatically published.

When Drupal 7.x is installed with the default installation profile, there are primarily two *content types* defined; *article* and *basic page*. Some other content types (e.g. blog, book, forum, poll) can be enabled on the modules administration page, where you will find other core and contributed modules. It is also possible to create your own content types.

1.7.16.1   Content types in Drupal 7.x core

- **Article.** In preceding Drupal versions, this content type is called *story*. The default Drupal 7.x installation profile enables the *article* content type as a default. Articles are information updated frequently and often categorized and cross referenced.
- **Basic page.** In preceding Drupal versions, this content type is simply called *page*. The default Drupal 7.x installation profile also enables the *basic page* content type as a default. Typically basic pages refer to static content that are usually linked into the main navigation bar (e.g. about us).
- **Blog entry.** The core blog module allows registered users on your site to create their own blogs. Every entry in a user blog belongs to the content type *blog entry*.
- **Book page.** *Book pages* are enabled by the core *book* module. This enables the creation of a collaborative book. Older versions of Drupal only permitted nodes of content type *book page* to be added to a book. In Drupal 7.x nodes of any content type can be made part of a book.
- **Forum.** Nodes posted in a *forum* are topics for a discussion and replies will be made as comments.
- **Poll.** A question that offers the site user a set of multiple choice responses is called a *poll*. It will automatically provide a progressive count of the number of received votes for each response.
- **Comment.** As previously mentioned, *comments* actually are not nodes, therefore a comment is never a content type. The comment module enables site users to post notes and replies to nodes and other comments on the site.

1.7.16.2   Content types in Drupal 5.x and 6.x core

The default content types in Drupal 5.x and 6.x are *story* and *page*. If you want to add custom fields to your content types in Drupal 5.x or 6.x, you will need to install the *Content Construction Kit (CCK)* which is a contributed module. The ability to create new fields is included in the core content types in Drupal 7.x.

Additional information beyond the Drupal defaults (title, body, authoring information, time created/updated, and publishing status) can also be gathered by defining custom fields. For instance, on a real estate site, a *Property* content type might have fields for the type of property, location, cost, etc.

1.7.16.3   Create your own content type

You might need to create your own content type as a way to further organize your site. You may do this by going to *Structure>Content types>Add content type*. For instance, you might decide to have ìLatest News and ìEditorials as two simple content types on a news publishing site, rather than just using ìArticleî for both.îî

1.8   Installing Drupal

You may install Drupal in two basic ways .The reckless way is to install straight to a live server, and the cautious way is to set up a test environment on your local computer so the entire world does not get to marvel at all your possible mistakes. If you know what you are doing though you can use latter method.

1.8.1   Obtaining Drupal installation scripts

The primary way to acquire Drupal installation scripts will be the official Drupal web site (www.drupal.org). You can also download additional modules for extending the functionality of your basic Drupal installation as well as additional themes to extend its look and feel. There are three basic download options to consider:

1.   Download directly from the Drupal repository using HTTP

2.   Download directly to your server using Secure Shell (SSH) access

3.   Download using a Concurrent Versions System (CVS) client

Some hosting servers provide a point and click installation using a program called "Fantastico". However, this installation method is usually provides an out-of-date release or may not meet your specific needs.

1.8.1.1   Downloading via the Drupal repository

The download page at the Drupal repository looks something like Figure 1.7.

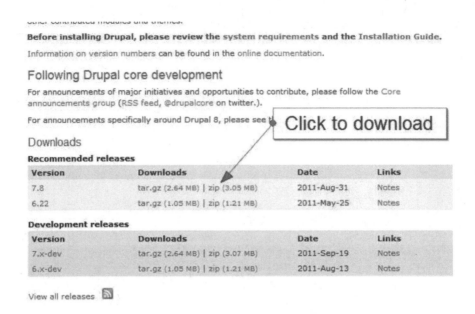

Figure 1.7   Downloading Drupal

Clicking on the link will start the download process for the release you have selected. Once the download is complete, you will need to unpackage (unzip or untar) the file into a development folder.

1.8.1.2   Downloading via SSH

If you need to do a direct download to an online server it may be faster to use SSH client access. In this case, right-click on the release you require, and click *copy link location*. You will get a link that looks something like http://ftp.drupal.org/files/projects/drupal-7.8.zip. Use the following procedure to download and decompress the file to a directory of your choice (drupalmodels is used in this example).

1.   In your SSH client open a new command line terminal

2.   Navigate to the desired installation directory or create a new one using the following commands.

    ```
    > Mkdir drupalmodels
    > Cd drupalmodels
    ```

3.   Use the *wget* command to download the archive file you need.

    ```
    >Wget http://ftp.drupal.org/files/projects/drupal-7.8.zip
    ```

4. Use the *unzip* command or an *untar* command to decompress the downloaded file.

```
>unzip drupal-7.8.zip
```

You may use the same procedure for downloading contributed modules and themes. In fact, SSH should make work a lot easier if there is need to download many new modules.

1.8.1.3   Downloading via CVS and Git

For more advanced programmers, there is the CVS option and the *Git* option. These options will not be discussed in any detail because they require the installation of third party programs and require higher level privileges to the Drupal repositories. You can apply for these privileges by registering as a user on the Drupal web site.

1.8.2   Installing Drupal on a local computer

There are a number of ways to setup a test environment on a local computer. Most developers who already know what they are doing or are installing from a tested *profile* will install and configure straight to a live server. However, there are several reasons to run the application first on a local development server, especially if you are doing developing a site from scratch.

■ A local development server enables you to work offline.
■ Everything published on the web is typically indexed and archived. So you may find your various http errors displayed on Google for quite longer than you would wish.

1.8.2.1   Installing on Windows computer

Windows is not a natural platform for running Drupal; it needs to run on a Linux platform. There are however, several ways to replicate the Linux environment on a Windows computer. Installing WampServer, enables you to run Apache, MySQL, and PHP in the Windows environment. WampserverI is available for free download at http://www.wampserver.com. The package includes the following components, which are preconfigured to work together.

■ Apache
■ MySQL
■ PHP

There are similar packages which also include Drupal distributions, but it is better to install WampServer, and then load it with the Drupal version of your choice.

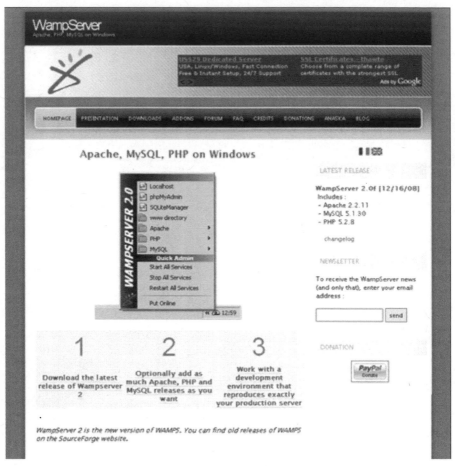

Figure 1.8   Downloading WampServer

WampServer self-installs. After you have unpacked the zip file, double click on the icon and follow the installation instructions. Your development environment should be ready in a few minutes (Figure 1.8).

1.8.2.2   Installing on Macintosh computer

Again, unless you are an advanced user or you just like a hard life, it is often better to use a pre-packaged solution such as MAMP, which works in much the same way as WampServer. MAMP may be downloaded at http://www.mamp.info/en/index.html.

1.8.2.3   Installing on Linux/Unix computer

Linux is the natural environment for Drupal. All that is needed to do is install PHP, MySQL and Apache. The methods available for doing this are quite technical and vary across the different flavors of these operating systems. Some good places to go for advice are:

- Installing PHP, MySQL and Apache under Linux, http://drupal.org/node/483
- XAMPP for Linux: http://drupal.org/node/115820

The second is particularly recommended as it employs a similar method to creating a development environment on PC and Mac.

1.8.2.4   Installing Drupal as a desktop application

Yet another option to setting up a Drupal development environment is to use one of the applications, which enable you to install Drupal just like you would a desktop application. This may be the easiest way to get your Drupal installation up and running in very little time.

One of the options is the Bitnami distribution, which enables you to install Drupal and the entire Apache, MySQL, and PHP stack as a point and click application on your desktop. You may download Bitnamiís Drupa distribution at http://bitnami.org/stack/drupal.l

Another similar application is the Acquia Dev Desktop,. This program also installs the entire stack, but with a version of Drupal distributed by a company called Acquia which includes some of the most common contributed modules and some pre-configuration. You may download the Acquia Dev Desktop at http://network.acquia.com/downloads.

1.8.3   Installing Drupal 6.x on localhost using WampServer

If you have opted to create a Drupal installation in a localhost environment instead of using a desktop application, here are the steps you should follow (Figure 1.9).

1. First, download the latest stable release of Drupal.
2. Locate the directory in which WampServer is installed on your computer—usually the root of your computer's main directory (C:\) and in a folder named Wamp. In the Wamp directory; find the www subdirectory and place your downloaded file in it.

3.   Unzip the Drupal download. This may require a tool such as Winzip.

4.   Rename the resulting Drupal folder whatever you like.

5.   Click on the WampServer icon on your desktop. After the server is running, ensure that *Start all Services* is selected.

6.   If you open a web browser and navigate to http://localhost, this will bring up the main WampServer panel and in it, you will see your Drupal project file under *Your Projects*.

7.   Drupal requires a database, so you must create one for your project. Clicking on the phpMyAdmin link, will bring up for the panel for pgpMyAdmin. Here you will enter the name of your new database in the *Create New Database* field. It may make sense to give your new database the same name as the project file to simplify things.

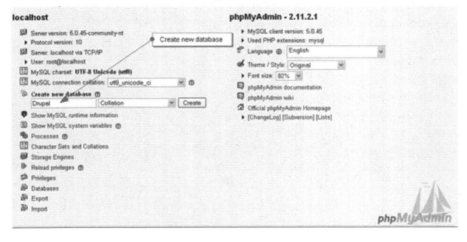

Figure 1.9   Creating a new database using phpMyAdmin

8.   Navigate to http://localhost/Drupal and start the installation (Figure 1.10). The automated installation script of Drupal will populate the database tables and applies the correct settings in the settings.php file. This installation script will also set other parameters such as the base URL, the database connection string, and create tables in the database.

9.   The rest of the installation is a simple step-by-step process. Correct any host-specific errors, and then proceed to the *Database Configuration* page (Figure 1.11).

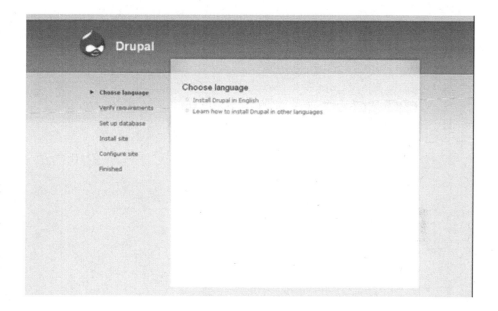

Figure 1.10   Installation start screen Drupal 6.x

10. On the database configuration page, add the following required parameters:

■ Database name: *xxxxx* (the name you have given to the database)

■ Database user name: *root* (unless it has been changed)

■ Database password: Leave blank (unless one was added when setting up the database)

■ Database host: *Localhost*

■ Database port: *Ignore this*

■ Table prefix: You may safely ignore this unless you are installing more than one instance of Drupal on a single database. Otherwise, the second Drupal instance will not install because the name of the tables will be similar. You may use a prefix such as DR2_ to distinguish between instances.

After completion, the installation success screen will be shown.

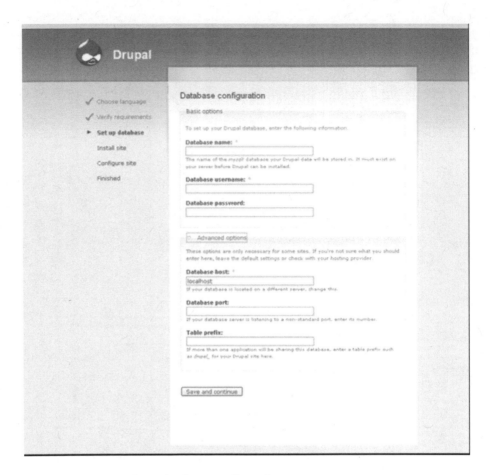

Figure 1.11   Drupal 6.x database configuration screen

1.8.4   Installing Drupal 7.x on localhost

The steps are roughly the same as installing Drupal 6.x, the difference being in the concluding steps. We will do the sequences all over again so the panes will be familiar; we will start from Step 8:

8.   Drupal has an automated installation script that automatically populates database tables and sets the correct settings in the settings.php file. The installation script will set the base URL, connect Drupal to the database, and create tables in the database. Navigate to your installation directory (http://localhost/[directory]) and start the installation (Figure 1.12).

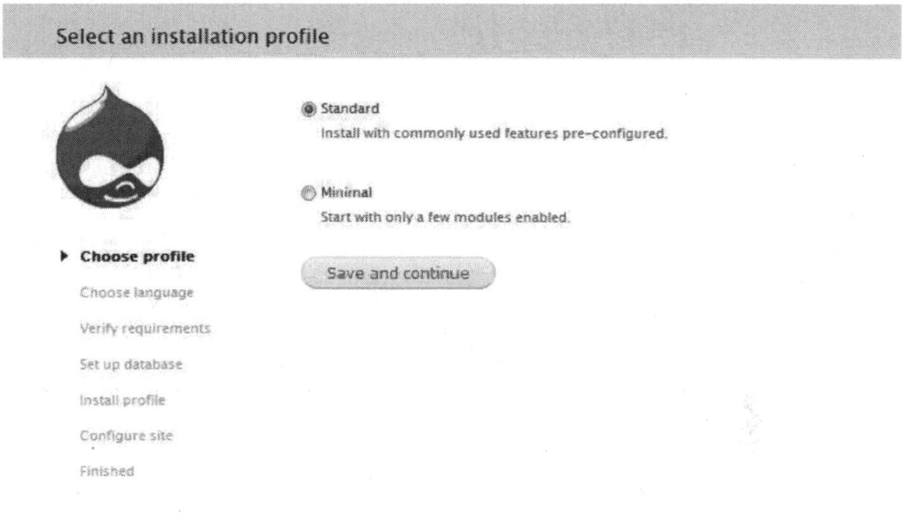

Figure 1.12   Installation start screen for Drupal 7.x

9.   The rest of the installation is a simple step-by-step process. Correct any host-specific errors, and then proceed to the *Database Configuration* page (Figure 1.13).

10.   In the Database Configuration page, add the following required parameters:

- Database name: *xxxxx* (the name you have given to the database)

- Database user name: *root* (unless it has been changed)

- Database password: Leave blank (unless one was added when setting up the database)

- Database host: *Localhost*

- Database port: *Ignore this*

Now click on *Save and Continue*. In few seconds, the installation screen will come up with a title *Configure Site*. This time though it also looks a little different from the previous version (Figure 1.14).

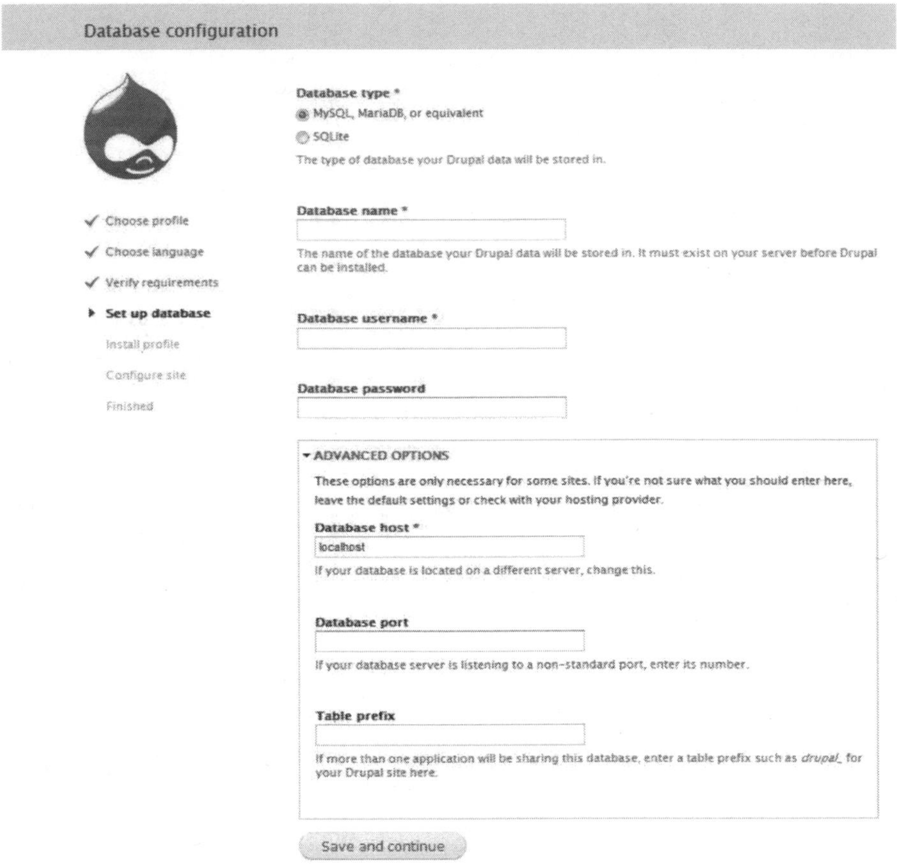

Database configuration

Database type *
- MySQL, MariaDB, or equivalent
- SQLite

The type of database your Drupal data will be stored in.

✓ Choose profile

✓ Choose language

✓ Verify requirements

▶ **Set up database**

Install profile

Configure site

Finished

Database name *

The name of the database your Drupal data will be stored in. It must exist on your server before Drupal can be installed.

Database username *

Database password

▼ ADVANCED OPTIONS

These options are only necessary for some sites. If you're not sure what you should enter here, leave the default settings or check with your hosting provider.

Database host *

localhost

If your database is located on a different server, change this.

Database port

If your database server is listening to a non-standard port, enter its number.

Table prefix

If more than one application will be sharing this database, enter a table prefix such as *drupal_* for your Drupal site here.

Save and continue

Figure 1.13   Database configuration screen Drupal 7.x

1.8.5   Installing Drupal on a remote live server

The steps for installing Drupal on a remote server are essentially the same as for installing on a local machine. As previously mentioned, some web hosting packages come with one-click installation tools such as *Fantastico*—a software application that automates the installation of web applications to a website (Figure 1.15). This sort of installation is prone to security problems relating to obsolescence and to spammers. It is usual for some hosting companies to share an update as soon as a new release is available to improve user experience and to heighten security. Usually though, as experienced Drupal developers know, it is wiser to wait until a new release is completely functional and has sufficient compatible modules.

Configure site

✓ Choose profile
✓ Choose language
✓ Verify requirements
✓ Set up database
✓ Install profile
▶ **Configure site**
Finished

SITE INFORMATION

Site name *

models

Site e-mail address *

you@yourdomain

Automated e-mails, such as registration information, will be sent from this address. Use an
address ending in your site's domain to help prevent these e-mails from being flagged as spam.

SITE MAINTENANCE ACCOUNT

Username *

admin

Spaces are allowed; punctuation is not allowed except for periods, hyphens, and underscores.

E-mail address *

timi@xceedia.co.uk

Password *

••••••••   Password strength: **Fair**

Confirm password *

••••••••   Passwords match: yes

To make your password stronger:
  • Add uppercase letters
  • Add numbers
  • Add punctuation

SERVER SETTINGS

Default country

United Kingdom ▾

Select the default country for the site.

Default time zone

Europe/London: Tuesday, September 20, 2011 - 16:38 +0100 ▾

By default, dates in this site will be displayed in the chosen time zone.

UPDATE NOTIFICATIONS

☑ Check for updates automatically

☑ Receive e-mail notifications

The system will notify you when updates and important security releases are available for
installed components. Anonymous information about your site is sent to Drupal.org.

(Save and continue)

Figure 1.14   Site information page Drupal 7.x

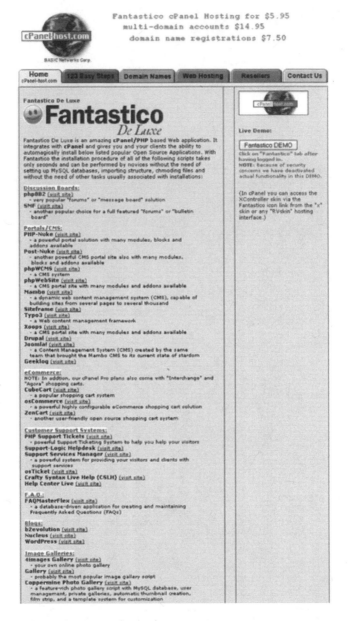

Figure 1.15 Fantastico control panel

1.9 Learning Drupal

Drupal is an extremely versatile framework but the learning curve may be quite daunting especially for persons used to other content management systems. However, for a developer this learning experience should pay off in the ability to create very flexible and adaptable web applications.

The following are resources help make it easier to learn Drupal:

- Drupalbasics
  http://drupalbasics.com/
- Geeks and god
  http://geeksandgod.com/podcast-series/building-a-website-with-drupal-cms
- SpryDev
  http://sprydev.com/category/sprydev-seo-podcast
- The Lullabot Drupal podcast
  http://www.lullabot.com/podcast
- The Acquia podcast series
  http://acquia.com/blog/introducing-acquia-podcast-series
- Drupal Dojo
  http://drupaldojo.com
- The Art Lab
  http://theartlab.net/podcast/drupal-school
- Minezone
  http://www.minezone.org/blog/2007/11/01
  /45-screencasts-to-get-you-kicking-ass-with-drupal
- Joomla Frequently Asked Questions (FAQ)
  http://drupal.org/faqs
- Drupal Forums
  http://drupal.org/forum

1.10   Summary

In this chapter, we learned the basic Drupal terminologies and terms of interests to both users and developers. We also learned about how to create an installation environment for Drupal and how to carry out the actual installation. The reader is given information on where to get further on-line resources for working with Drupal.

Chapter 2

Adding, Classifying and Viewing Content

In the last chapter, we learned how to install and configure Drupal. We introduced content and content types. In reiteration, content can be any kind of material that you put on your site, including text, images, video, audio, and any electronic file items. Content types are classifications, which describe the structure of a particular set of content and how that content is created and displayed. Drupal 7 installs with seven different ready to use content types—basic page, article, blog, poll, comment, book, and forum. We also learned the basic structure of a Drupal framework.

In this chapter, we will be learning how to create content, using the pre-defined *Content type* template forms. We will also be learning how to classify content using the *Taxonomy module*. Additionally we will be learning how to take an existing static HTML site and convert it to Drupal.

The importance of this chapter is that it should help the reader understand how Drupal works, and how things are placed in the Drupal framework, as a basis for getting Drupal to work as expected for their own projects. Without this chapter, it may not be easy for new users to navigate the Drupal development ocean.

The section on migrating a static site to Drupal takes into account that most businesses already have a rudimentary static site, which could benefit from the ease and lower cost of maintenance afforded by a dynamic content management system such as Drupal. The objective of that section is to assist in performing such migrations with greater ease and in less time.

Below are other highlights of this chapter:

- How to create content in Drupal?
- How to describe, classify and organize content by use of taxonomy.
- How to port an existing static HTML site into a Drupal framework.

2.1   Adding your first posts

The most basic task users need to accomplish on a Drupal site is to add and display content. When a Drupal site is implemented, a user with administrative privileges will be presented with the following screen (Figure 2.1). Click the *Add new content* link to display the *Add content* screen.

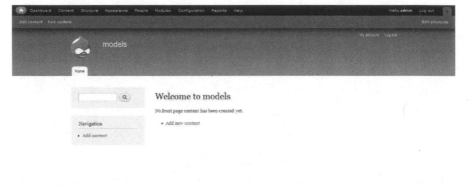

Figure 2.1   New site front page

Choose the type of content to add for the first post. The title of the post is *About this site*. To do this, click on the *Add new content* link to bring up the *Add content* screen (Figure 2.2). Click on the *Basic page* content link, which will bring up a form as shown in Figure 2.3.

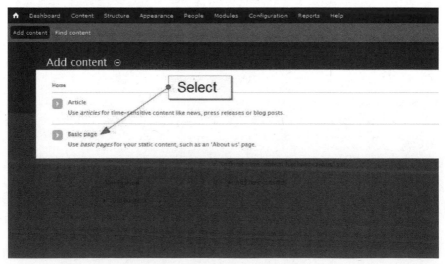

Figure 2.2   Link to Basic page content type

2.1.1   Add, post and link a menu

Now we add some text content as follows. Some fields are not compulsory so letís ignore them at this time. However, we must add content to fields *Title* and *Body* (Figure 2.3).

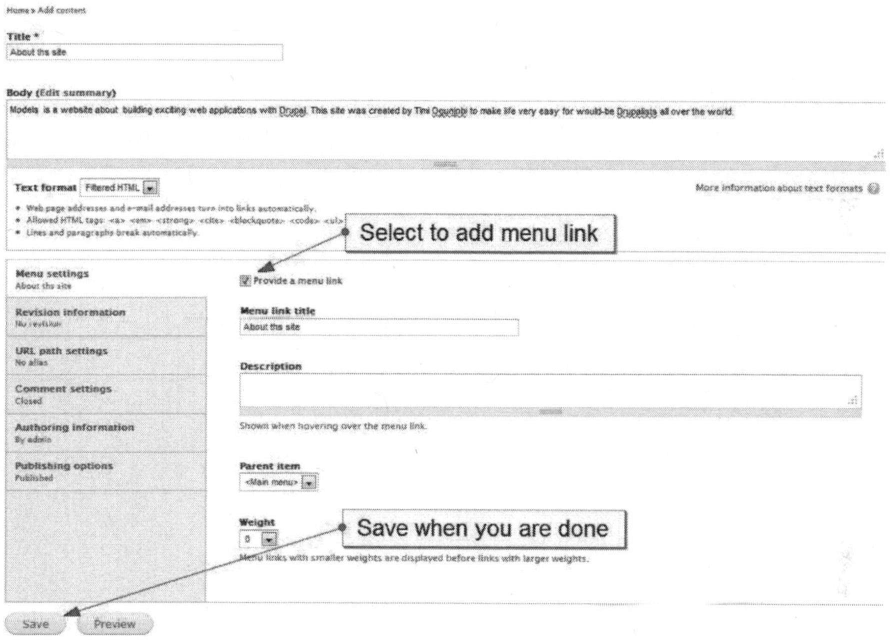

Figure 2.3   Adding content and linking to a menu

After adding the page title and the body, add a menu link to the page and link it to the Main mcnu. We shall see the result of this in Figure 2.5.

At the bottom, left side of the form (Figure 2.4), select the tab which reads *Publishing options*. Make sure *Published* is selected. Ordinarily you will need to select the *Promoted to front page* option if you want this post to appear on the front page but in a new Drupal installation, your first post always goes to the front page.

After saving, your front page now looks like the following and you should see the *About this site* menu tab at the top (Figure 2.5).

Note there is a *Home* tab, which also points to the *About this site* page. If in the future you decide to create another page, the *Home* page will automatically change.

Figure 2.4   Selecting publishing options

Figure 2.5   Created page and menu link in primary menu

2.2   Viewing and editing a node

In Drupal, viewing a page and editing a page are almost the same , assuming you have permissions on the site to edit. Looking at Figure 2.5, there are two tabs at the top of the post: *view* and *edit*. This unique feature of Drupal makes it possible for roles with sufficient permission, to simultaneously edit and see the front end without having to switch to the administrative back end like in other content management systems. With Drupal and for permitted roles, there is only one single user interface.

Authenticated users with appropriate permissions will see *edit* tabs above their nodes while anonymous users will not. That is often the only difference between the editor and user experience.

People who have never used a CMS are often much less confused about this approach than people who have previously used systems where the input screens look very different from the output screens. It is an unlearning thing.

2.3   Drupal taxonomy

Taxonomy can be described as the practice of classifying things. In Drupal, the taxonomy module is an important piece of the sites' information architecture.

Taxonomy may be thought of as the use of *categories* for describing content. In earlier versions of Drupal, it was called *categories*. By using the taxonomy feature, you are able to gather content under one term or another.

2.3.1   Drupal taxonomy functions

Taxonomy gives a Drupal site the ability to use organizational keywords otherwise called categories, tags, or metadata. In Drupal, these keywords can be grouped together under *vocabularies*. The taxonomy module provides the means of creation, management, and application of those vocabularies.

2.3.2   Planning taxonomies

The following steps are used to establish taxonomy in Drupal:

1.   Decide on a new *vocabulary* name.

2. List the terms that should be associated within the *vocabulary* and determine their general relationships. The arrangement can be flat (as in a tagging system), or hierarchical, with parents and children.

To get to the *taxonomy* design page click *Structure>Taxonomy.* For example, this is how you may want to create a taxonomy for a site with content relating to Athletics:

```
Vocabulary=Athletics
    term=track
        child-term=100m hurdles
        child-term=100m dash
    term=field
        child-term=discus throw
        child-term=pole vault
```

To create this taxonomy, click the *Add vocabulary* link on the *Taxonomy* screen (Figure 2.6) and add this information:

```
Name: Athletics
Description: Whatever you like
```

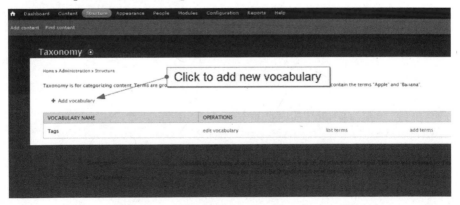

Figure 2.6   Adding new vocabulary

On the *Taxonomy* screen (Figure 2.7) which shows up click on the *add terms* link to add your terms (i.e., field; track).

You will add the child-terms, if such exists, just the same way as you would the terms but with a little extra detail. You link the child term to its

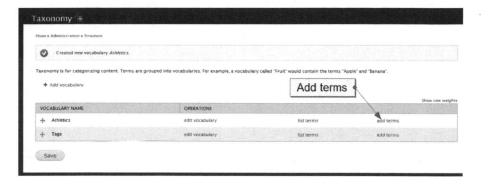

Figure 2.7   Adding terms to vocabulary

parent term by clicking in the *Relations>Parent terms* field, and select its parent term(s) as follows (Figure 2.8):

Home » Administration » Structure » Taxonomy » Athletics

Name *

100m dash

Description

teaches how to run very fast especially when a dog is chasing you

Text format Filtered HTML

- Web page addresses and e-mail addresses turn into links automatically.
- Allowed HTML tags: `<a> <em> <strong> <cite> <blockquote> <code> <ul> <ol> <li> <dl> <dt> <dd>`
- Lines and paragraphs break automatically.

More

URL alias

Optionally specify an alternative URL by which this term can be accessed. Use a relative path and don't add a trailing slash or the URL alias won't work.

▾ RELATIONS   • select parent term

Parent terms

`<root>`
field
track

Figure 2.8   Relating taxonomy terms

Note that several levels of taxonomy can be created just by relating a new child term to a parent term. After you have added all the predetermined terms, this is what the resulting taxonomy tree should look like (Figure 2.9).

The above procedure creates a controlled vocabulary, in which content authors are able to assign terms to content which they subsequently create. In Drupal 7, vocabularies may be assigned to content types by means of a *term reference* field for that content type. The way to set up the term reference field is to choose the vocabulary from which the term will be chosen.

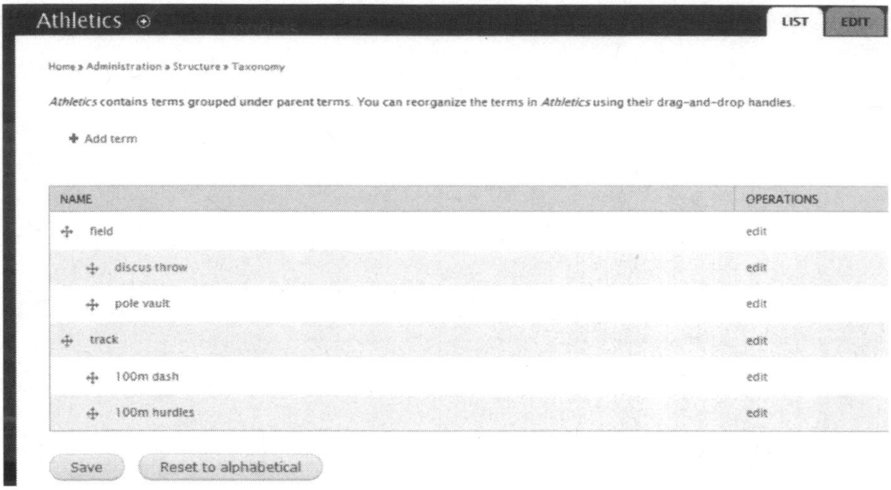

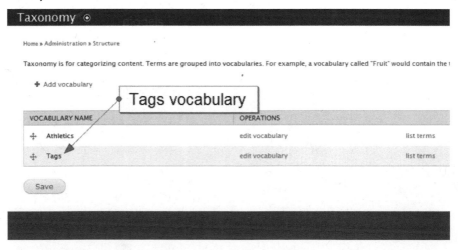

Figure 2.9   Sample taxonomy tree

Alternatively, user-defined *Tags*, may be permitted. This will enable the addition of a term to Drupal content on the fly. In Drupal 7, this ready to use vocabulary is included by default in content types (Figure 2.10). Therefore, users can immediately add tags or terms to their content without the need to create new vocabularies. However, for some content types, especially if newly created, the administrator will need to enable the tags vocabulary by the term reference procedure.

If multiple vocabularies are attached to a content type it is possible to classify content in an almost limitless fashion.

Figure 2.10   The Tags vocabulary

2.3.3   General principles that apply to the Drupal taxonomy module

- Each vocabulary describes a set of terms unless the vocabulary is a Tag type where the user manually inserts terms.
- An unlimited number of vocabularies can be included in a site to classify content.
- An associated *id number* is allocated by Drupal to every vocabulary and each taxonomy term.
- There is no limit to the number of terms that a vocabulary can contain.
- Vocabularies can be arranged into a hierarchy without taking additional steps. Terms can also be ordered into hierarchies within a vocabulary.
- In Drupal 7, the *Tags* vocabulary never needs to be predefined in order to create a tagging vocabulary. In Drupal 6, this has to be achieved by designating *free tagging* or *tags* and choosing *multiple select*.
- Vocabularies can be set to allow terms to have *related terms in* Drupal 6. Related terms can be compared with "*See also*" in a thesaurus or dictionary. This can be replicated in Drupal 7 by adding a *term reference* field to the vocabulary.
- In Drupal 6, vocabularies can attach multiple terms to a node. This will be determined in the process of creating the vocabulary. In Drupal 7 however, this is determined while setting each *term reference* field.

2.3.4   Guidelines for taxonomy design

With small sites, where the content can be described by a handful of terms, the taxonomy scheme is usually easy to set up. However, in larger projects, good taxonomy design can be the difference between an intuitive site and an information architecture nightmare. The *views* module (which few sites can do without) relies heavily on taxonomy. Here are some general rules for good taxonomy design:

- **Keep it simple.** If a vocabulary is not well known to users, keep it below 40 terms. An example of a well-known vocabulary is the list of all countries in the world.

- **Be careful with the relationships.** An unwieldy parent-child scheme is often a result of poor design. If your taxonomy relies on these structures, think about segregating the vocabulary. Use parent-child relationships with caution.
- **Never assume intuitiveness.** Site users are not experts on taxonomy, not even if they designed it on their own. Therefore, create terms that are adequately described and easy to understand.
- **Taxonomy could present legacy problems.** Apart from adding more vocabularies and terms, once you have a load of tagged data, it is hard to make changes to a site's taxonomy structures, and nobody is likely to go back and edit existing data.
- **Taxonomy is not an exact science.** As soon as data is added to a new site, you will often find flaws, and need to further refine. Much of good taxonomy is actually a matter of trial and error.

2.4   Moving a static site to Drupal

What is the difference between a static and dynamic site? A static site is one coded in HTML only. Each page of a static site is a separate document, which means that you may only edit the site by individually editing the HTML code in each document.

A dynamic site is coded differently and more amenable to the separation of site structure and site content. Each page is dynamically constructed on the basis of information in a database. The information in the database is normally edited by the use of a forms interface. A major benefit of dynamic sites is they allow you to easily change only the data content of the site and not the front-end designówhich may be a huge relief when you have a site with hundreds of pages and you need to change just the header. Also, with a dynamic site, new pages can be easily added on the fly.

2.4.1   Moving to Drupal

Converting a static site to Drupal is, simply put, premised upon common sense. The simple step is to just take your content and work it into Drupal. This is true for an existing site of no more than a few dozen pages, but when you have a site running into hundreds of pages, it may be a bit more complicated. Fortunately, there are some clever modules, which could reduce the pain for the developer.

In any case, here are a few steps, which should ensure that things go as intended.

2.4.2   Enable clean URLs within Drupal

A new Drupal install will always emit strange URLs such as
http://www.mysite.com/?q=node/1. Obviously, your old site will not have pages addressed in this way. To clean up the URL, go to *Configuration>Clean URLs* (Figure 2.11).

This will prompt Drupal to run a script to ascertain whether your server settings will permit this feature. If the test passes, *Clean URLs* is affected on your site and the above example should read like
http://www.mysite.com/node/1. Unfortunately, this is unlikely to work in localhost mode.

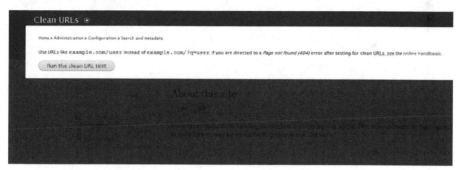

Figure 2.11   Clean URLs page

2.4.3   The Pathauto module

The URL shown above does not look a lot like what you will want to see. For example, suppose you have a page titled *Our Services*. When you copy the content to Drupal, you will likely get something like http://www.mysite.com/node/1, which is hardly descriptive. There are several ways to change the URL manually. However, installing the *Pathauto* module makes short work of creating plain-language titles for your pages. The *Pathauto* module will dynamically generate path aliases for site content (including nodes, vocabulary, users, etc.) without the users needing to manually specify the path alias.

2.4.4   How to install and select new modules

All your installed modules are located on the *Modules* page (*Home>Administration>Modules*). However, with a new installation of Drupal, the *Modules* page only contains the core modules. For example, the *Pathauto* module will not be there.

Installing new modules is easier with Drupal 7 than in earlier versions. However, you will need to go to the modules directory on the Drupal web site. Search for the *Pathauto* module the same way as we did while installing Drupal. Copy the download link, this time for the *tar* archive. Click on the *Install new module* link near the top of the modules page of your site and paste the link into the *Install from a URL* field (Figure 2.12).

Alternatively, if you have the *tar* file on your computer, you may use the *Upload a module of theme archive to install* option to perform the installation. Before the *Pathauto* module can be installed and enabled, it will require the *Token module*, which you may install in the same way.

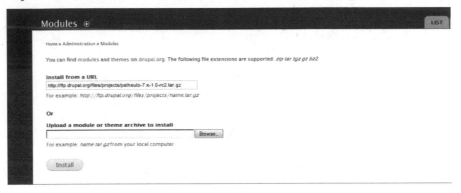

Figure 2.12   Install from a URL field

2.4.5   The WYSIWYG module

This module permits users to do a WYSIWYG edit of site pages directly. It can make life a lot easier for the site administrator and users, especially if they don't know HTML. Look for this module in the modules directory of the Drupal website. Like the *Pathauto* module, it will also have a dependent module, which you need to install.

2.4.6   Set up taxonomy/terms to reflect the existing folder structure

First, you will need to make a note of all existing URLs and replicate them within Drupal. If the present static site is of less than a couple of dozen pages or so, this may not be so much a problem. You merely need to determine your menu structure and create content accordingly.

Larger sites may require setting up elaborate taxonomy structures and using the *Views* module to expose the content in a manner closest to the original structure.

2.4.7   How to install and select a theme

Themes are installed and selected in the same way as modules. In this case, however, you will find the *Themes* page by selecting *Appearance* from the top *Administration* menu bar. This will display the enabled themes, together with thumbnail images of how they look (Figure 2.13).

Figure 2.13   Installing new theme

If you don't particularly like any of the installed themes, take a trip to the Drupal web site and go to the themes directory page. Trawl the directory until you find some that are close to what you want your site to look like. Again, copy the URL location of the tar file and upload it as we did earlier for new modules.

2.4.8   Setting up a menu

Recall when we created content for the first page (*About this site*) on the demonstration site, we had a choice of putting a menu link to this page from the *Main Menu*. We can also create menu links in the *Main Menu* for all the top-level site pages. In this example, letíscreate a secondary link to the *About this site* page and call it *Contact site administrator* (Figure 2.14). Also, recall how we created sub-terms in the taxonomy; we will be doing something similar here.

1.   Click on the *Add content* link and create another basic page.

2.   Enter your desired Menu link title.

3.   Near the bottom, as you select *Provide a menu link*.

4.   You will also find a drop-down prompting you to select a *Parent item*. In this case select *About this site* as the parent item

5.   Repeat for all other pages on your site, according to the menu structure of your old static site.

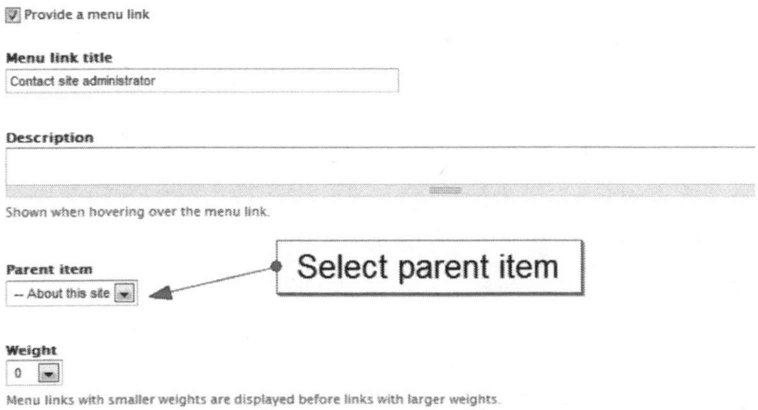

Figure 2.14   Linking two menu items

2.4.9 Copying text from browser

Copying content from the old site can be easily done by opening pages in the browser, selecting the content with your mouse, and pasting it in your new Drupal page. However, in doing this it is unlikely that you will be able to preserve page formatting, embedded images and other media. For simple sites with few pages though it may be the quickest way, and modules such as WYSIWYG can greatly assist with formatting. If you're going to try the old cut and paste method it is strongly recommended that you also install a *WYSIWYG* module such as the *TinyMCE* module to assist with the formatting.

2.4.10 Copying raw formatted html

Alternatively, you may consider viewing the source code for the page as shown in a browser and copying/pasting the relevant HTML code into the newly created Drupal page. This should retain much of the old formatting. For this to work successfully, you may need to select *Full HTML* (Figure 2.15) from the *Text format* dropdown, when you paste, if it is not your default format.

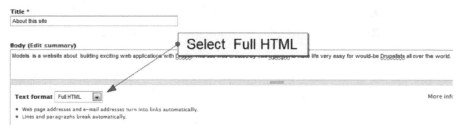

Figure 2.15   Full HTML option

2.4.11 Path to images and other web assets

Finally, if your old static website has images, links to document files and other media included, such media already resided somewhere within the web space or on a remote server. For example, let's assume they are located in a folder called …*assets* within the root web directory

In this case, if your Drupal development has been done in the assets folder, you need not worry. Otherwise, you will need to create a similar directory in your new root and import the old files into it. This is far from the how Drupal organizes and stores files, images and other media, but it should get you on your way.

2.5   Summary

In this chapter, we learned how to add new content to a Drupal site and how to describe, classify, and organize content on the site by using the *Taxonomy module*. We also learned how to create an effective taxonomy structure. Finally, we learned how to port an existing static HTML site into the Drupal framework.

Chapter 3

Administering Drupal

In the previous chapter we learned about Drupal terminology, features and components, how to create content and how to move a static web site into a dynamic Drupal framework. The objective was to give users a basic overview of how Drupal functions and how to integrate it into their present web development strategies.

In this chapter, we examine how to administer a Drupal web site in the context of menu configuration, content management, user management, site backup and restoration, publishing a site, performance, and security.

This chapter is important because it will enable users to achieve competence in the following areas:

- Navigation and usage of the *Administrative toolbar*
- Site backup and restoration to forestall possible disaster
- Publication/migration techniques (local to server, server to server, etc.)
- Site performance and security enhancement techniques.

The sections on site backup/restoration, publication, and security take into cognizance accidents that can inadvertently occur on a live site, which could make the site unserviceable. These sections demonstrate how to forestall and/or recover from such occurrences.

3.1 Administration overview

As an administrator, you and whomever has administrative permissions on the site have unique privileges; primarily the ability to manipulate site behavior via the administration back end. The administration pages contain the tools to configure and alter the look and feel of the site.

After the successful installation of a Drupal site, the person who performed the installation will be granted administrative privileges and identified with a user ID of 1 or user/1. By default, the administrator has privileges to manage the content, functionality, and role-based user permissions of the site.

3.1.1   The administrative toolbar

When installing a Drupal site, you are given the choice of what installation profile to use. Unless a minimal profile was selected during the installation process, you should see the *Administrative* toolbar at the top of the *Administration* page, (Figure 3.1). Under the *Administrative* toolbar, you will find another bar. This short-cut bar can make the site a lot easier to administer because it makes related features are conveniently selectable via a single interface.

Figure 3.1   The Administrative toolbar

The *Administrative* toolbar and *Shortcuts* bar (Section 3.1.4) can be removed by disabling their associated module via the Modules administration page (*Administration>Modules*) or going to http://mysite.com/admin/modules. If the toolbar is disabled, you can reach the administrative screens directly by following this link http://mysite.com/admin.

If the appropriate module links are enabled and visible, the following sections describe the functionality of each of the options available on the *Administrative* toolbar.

3.1.1.1   Home icon

Clicking the *Home* icon (situated at the left end of the toolbar), will take you to the front page. The home icon link makes it possible to preview any changes made in the administrative back end from a front page perspective (Figure 3.2).

Figure 3.2   The Home icon

3.1.1.2   Dashboard

The *Dashboard* link displays a customizable overview of important site information, such as recent content and newly registered users to administrators (Figure 3.3). Alternatively, the *Dashboard* is accessible at this link http://www.mysite.com/admin/dashboard.

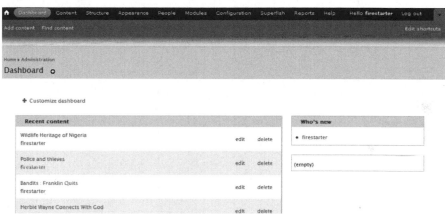

Figure 3.3   Administration Dashboard

3.1.1.3   Content

The *Content* link takes you to the *Content* page (Figure 3.4) where administrators can find and manage site content, comments, and create new pages.

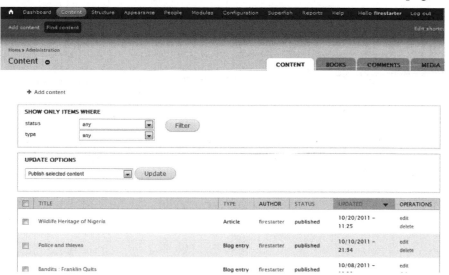

Figure 3.4   Content administration page

3.1.1.4   Structure

The *Structure* link displays the *Structure* page (Figure 3.5) from which you will find tools to edit blocks, define new content types, configure menus, taxonomies, and to configure contributed modules and several other tasks.

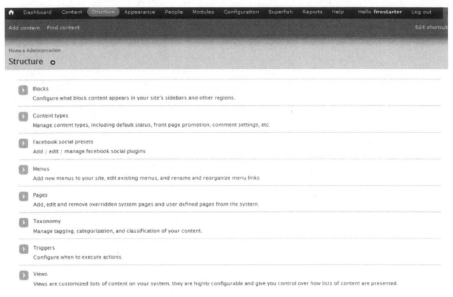

Figure 3.5   Structure administration page

3.1.1.5   Appearance

The *Appearance* link takes you to the *Appearance* page (Figure 3.6) which enables you to change the general appearance of the web site. From the page, you may switch between themes, install themes, and update existing themes.

3.1.1.6   People

The *People* link takes you to the *People* page (Figure 3.7) where you manage the site's existing users. From this page, you may manually approve new users and you may block and delete old users. You may also manually create new user accounts.

3.1.1.7   Modules

The *Modules* link takes you to the *Modules* page (Figure 3.8) which shows a list of the installed modules on the web site. Here you may also update, enable, disable, and install new modules.

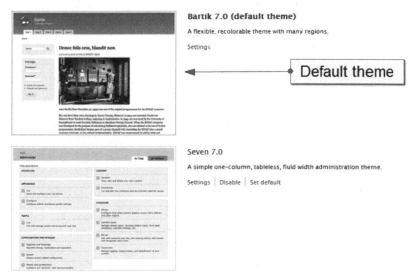

Home » Administration

Set and configure the default theme for your website. Alternative themes are available.

ENABLED THEMES

Bartik 7.0 (default theme)

A flexible, recolorable theme with many regions.

Settings

Default theme

Seven 7.0

A simple one-column, tableless, fluid width administration theme.

Settings │ Disable │ Set default

DISABLED THEMES

Garland 7.0

A multi-column theme which can be configured to modify colors and switch between fixed and fluid width layouts.

Enable │ Enable and set default

Stark 7.0

This theme demonstrates Drupal's default HTML markup and CSS styles. To learn how to build your own theme and override Drupal's default code, see the Theming Guide.

Enable │ Enable and set default

Figure 3.6   Themes administration page

3.1.1.8   Configuration

The *Configuration* link takes you to the *Configuration* page (Figure 3.9) where you will be able to alter the settings for various functionality, including contributed modules. You can also find tools to change general site information, user account settings, and settings for several other general administrative tasks.

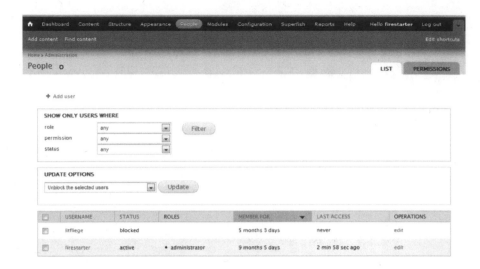

Figure 3.7   Users administration page

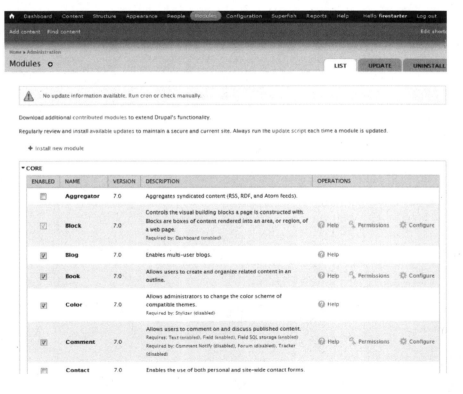

Figure 3.8   Modules administration page

3.1.1.9   Reports

The *Reports* link takes you to the *Reports* page (Figure 3.10) which provides tools for the checking the general health of the site. It will has links to pages such as the *Status report* page and others, which display information about site activity, site security and about necessary updates required for optimum performance of the site. Although some of the information brought up on this page may not look important, it is wise to address them anyway. Ignor-

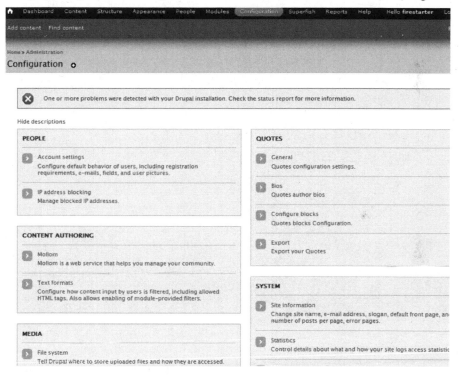

Figure 3.9   Site configuration page

ing them could be like ignoring a red light flashing in your car dashboard.

3.1.1.10   Help

The *Help* link will display the *Help* page which provides a list containing useful links for configuring and customizing the web site, adding functionality including modules and themes, etc. This page also provides a short glossary of help topics (Figure 3.11).

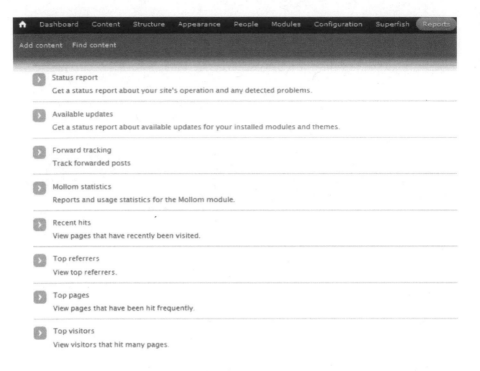

Figure 3.10   Reports page

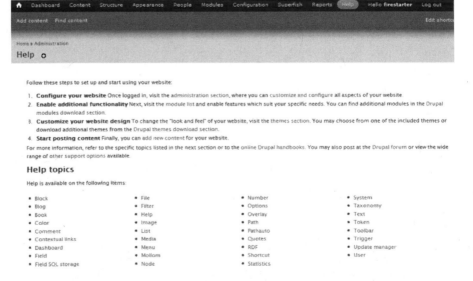

Figure 3.11   Help page

3.1.2   The Shortcut Bar

The *Shortcut* bar is enabled by the *Shortcut* module and it is the grey bar below the *Administrative* toolbar. It is useful for creating links to commonly-used pages within your site. By default, two links are available in the *Shortcut* bar: *Add content* and *Find content*. All shortcuts can be edited by clicking the *Edit shortcuts* link (Figure 3.12).

Figure 3.12   The shortcut bar

You can customize different sets of shortcuts from the page http:// mysite.com/admin/config/user-interface/shortcut/. Each user can select which set they would like to see on their user profile, or displayed as a block in any region, by adding the *Shortcuts* block to a region on the *Blocks* administration page (*Administration>Structure>Blocks*) or by navigating to this page http://mysite.com/admin/structure/block.

3.2   Basic site administration

An administrator should complete some basic housekeeping tasks after the Drupal site is ready and running. The following sections describe a few of them.

3.2.1   Status reports

As mentioned earlier, the Status report page (Figure 3.13) is a very important page, which shows any problems detected during the installation that should be addressed to ensure the site will function properly. Neglecting the warnings and errors may have dire consequences and prevent the optimum operation of the site. To check the status of the site, navigate to the *Reports>Status report* page from the *Administrative* toolbar, or go to http:// mysite.com/admin/reports/status.

In interpreting the site *Status report*, items with a red background are errors, which need immediate attention. You may also get warnings if there are scripts that need updating. The page will often display a message that "*Cron has not run*", with an option to run it manually because *cron* is configured to run automatically by default. This message is normal. *Cron.php* is a

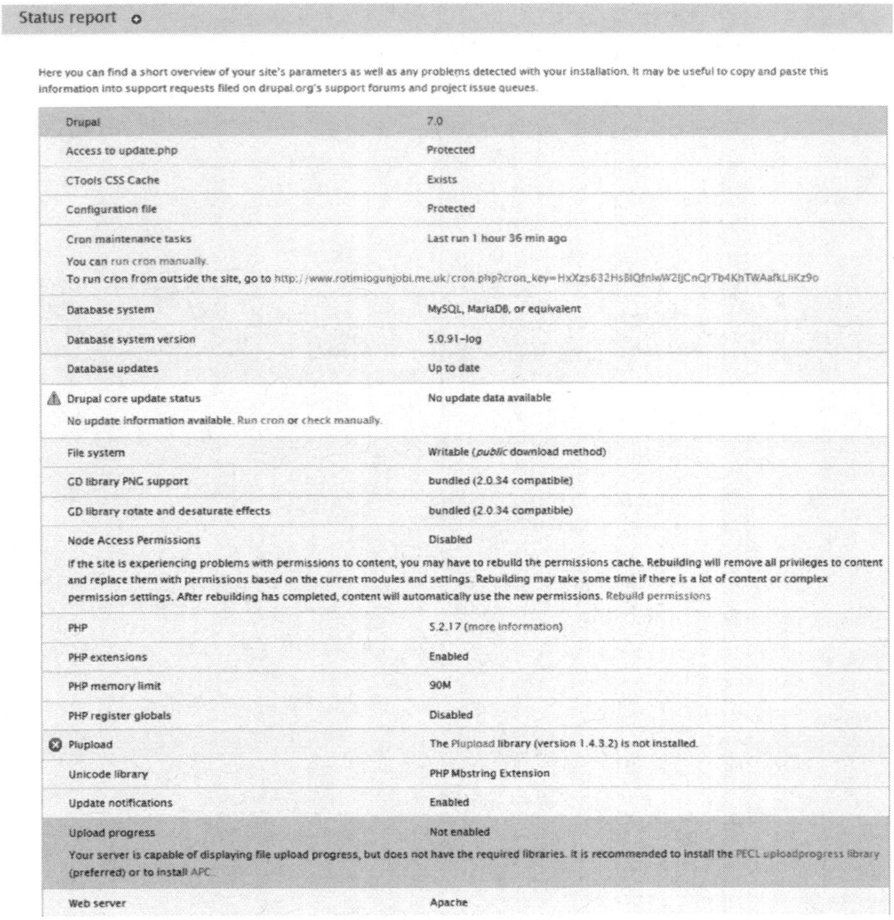

Figure 3.13   Status report page

script that needs to be run regularly to update your site content and for your site to continue functioning properly.

3.2.2   Site information

The *Site information* page (Figure 3.14) permits you to change some of your site's basic settings, such as the default front page path and the site name. The site information page can be accessed by navigating to the *Administration>Configuration>Site information* page or by going to http://mysite.com/admin/config/system/site-information.

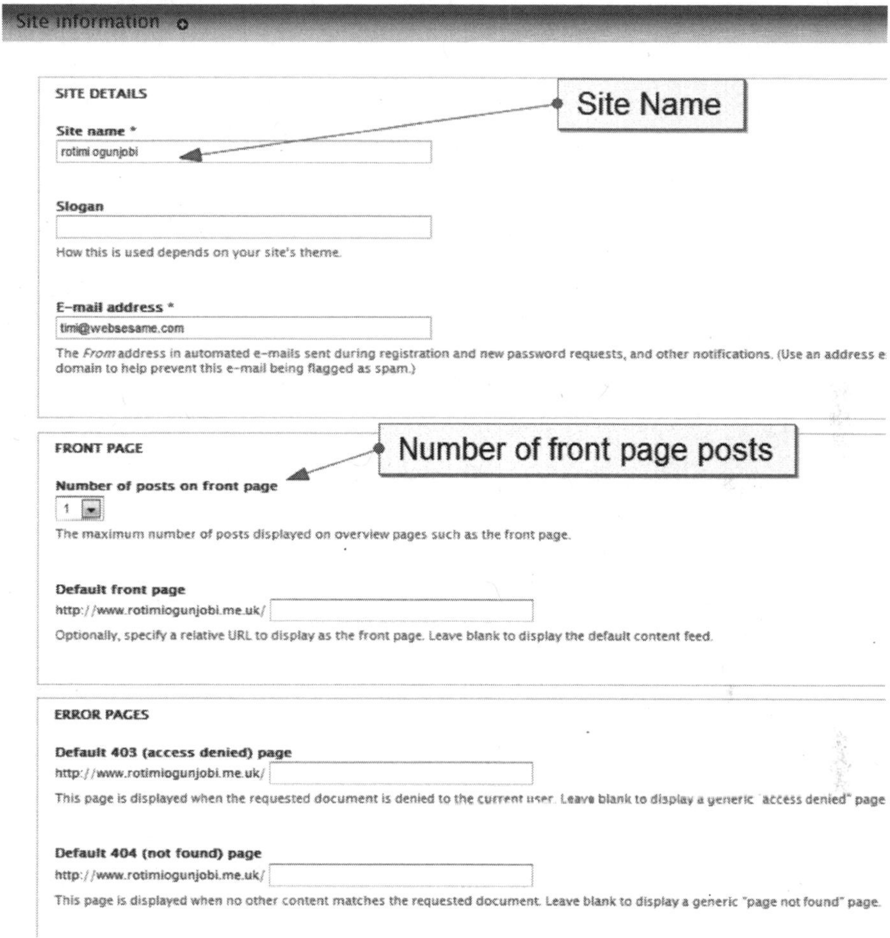

Figure 3.14   Editing site information

3.2.3   Site appearance

As we earlier learned, site appearance refers to the visual properties of the site, or more commonly the *look*. Site appearance can be changed by installing new themes or editing theme settings. To do any of this, navigate to the *Appearance* administration page at *Administer>Appearance* or go to following link http://mysite.com/admin/appearance.

3.2.4   Contextual links

Contextual links allow privileged users to perform tasks that are related to regions of the page without the need to go to the *Administration Dashboard*.

For example, when the mouse hovers over a block or node, a wheel-like link will be displayed (Figure 3.15) and when clicked, it initiates an *Ajax* function which will permit you make changes to the block or node without going to admin page.

Figure 3.15   Editing with contextual links

Contextual links is a default feature but it needs to be enabled in the *Modules* page to function. The user roles, which have permission to view and use contextual links, must be specified by the administrator. This can be done from the *Permissions* page (*People>Permissions*). If a user does not have permission to perform the specific action represented by the link, then *Contextual links* will not be displayed. If for example, the user does not have permission to edit nodes, *Contextual links* are not visible for nodes.

3.2.5   The Administrative overlay

Just like *Contextual links* make it possible to edit single elements more quickly, the *Administrative overlay* makes it possible to administer the entire Drupal site more quickly. Rather than entirely replacing the page in the browser window, the *Administrative overlay* employs JavaScript to display another administrative page as a layer over the current page. The *close* link on the overlay returns the user to the page being viewed before the link was clicked. As is the case with *Contextual links*, a user must have the permission to use *access overlay* in order to be able to see the administrative page as an overlay.

The *Overlay* module is enabled by default in a *Standard installation*, and can be disabled in the *Modules* page. Figure 3.16 shows the *Content* administration page using the *Administrative overlay*.

Figure 3.16   The overlay window

3.3   Content management

As we have learned in previous chapters, content refers to all the data posted to the site including nodes of all types as well as comments. With a standard installation, Drupal 7 has two default content types enabled; *Articles* and a *Basic page*. *Articles* is the content type generally used for creating content that is frequently updated .The *Basic page* content type is on the other hand generally used for posting the equivalent of static pages which may never need updating. Some other content types such as *Blog* and *Forum* can be enabled by enabling the corresponding modules in the *Modules* administration page.

Custom content types can also be newly created by clicking the *Add content type* link at the top of the *Content types* administration page (*Administration>Structure>Content types*) shown in Figure 3.17 or by navigating to http://mysite.com/admin/structure/types.

Go to the *Content* administration page (*Administration>Content)* or navigate to http://mysite.com/admin/content to be able to view a list of the site's current content. To add new content to the site click the *Add new content* link at the top.

3.3.1   Managing nodes

In the *Content* administration page, you are able to perform a variety of operations either on one node or simultaneously on several nodes. For example, you may publish or delete nodes, and you may promote or demote them from the front page. You may delete one or more nodes make a node

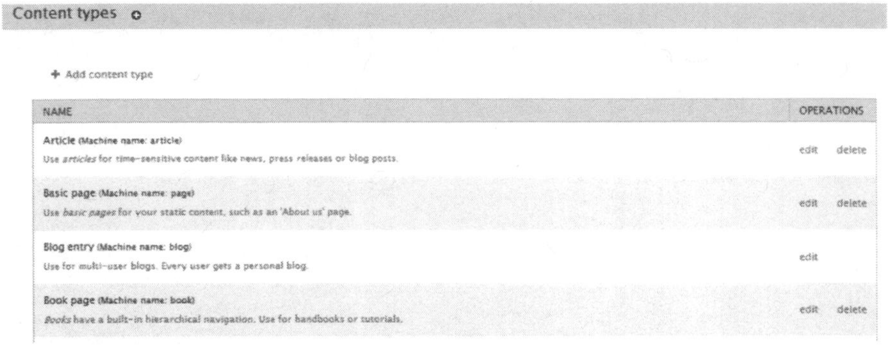

Figure 3.17   The Content types administration page

sticky at the top of lists. The *Content* administration page where you can do this can be accessed at *Administration>Content.*

From this administration page you may choose to edit content in several ways, and you may filter the content displayed by status, type or category for simultaneous operations such as bulk deleting of nodes which have been selected by the filter criteria..

3.3.2   Managing comments

Comments as we already know are not nodes, and so they are not displayed on the *Content* page along with all the nodes. However, A list view of comments to nodes can be displayed in the *Comments* page by going to *Administration>Content>Comments* (Figure 3.18) or by navigating to http://mysite/admin/content/comment. From the list you can choose to publish or unpublish one or more comments.

3.3.3   Managing URL paths

The path to site content is the URL, which is shown in the browser when the content is called up. By default, Drupal automatically creates web addresses web addresses like http://www.mysite.com/?q=node/419, which is not user friendly. Search engines don't think highly of them either and will give better rankings to pages that have friendly URLs, such as http://www.mysite.com/?q=about-our-widgets.

The core Path module lets you optionally create URL aliases for your Drupal pages. To use the *Path* module, it must be enabled. After enabling this module, whenever users with the right permissions create or edit

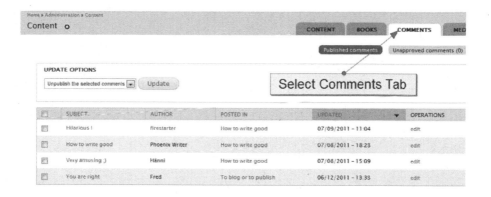

Figure 3.18   Comments administration page

posts, they will see a field for *URL alias*, where they may enter an alias of their choice (Figure 3.19).

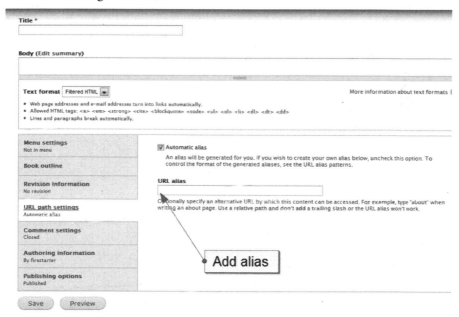

Figure 3.19   Aliasing content URL

On the *URL aliases* page, at *Administration>Configuration>Search and metadata>URL aliases* in Drupal 7 you will see a list of all the URL aliases on your site. There you can edit them, and add new ones. You can also assign more than one alias to a page. In Drupal 6, this feature is found at *Administration>Site building>URL aliases*.

By using Drupal's *clean URLs* feature, the alias you created (such as http://www.mysite.com/?q=about-our-widgets) is cleaned of the unnecessary bits and will become http://www.mysite.com/about-our-widgets; which is easier for users and site engines to work with.

3.3.4   Automatically generating URL path aliases with Pathauto

The purpose of the *Pathauto* module is to automate the generation of URL aliases. It will create automatic path aliases for nodes, users, and category terms. The aliases are generated when content is created on your site and each alias will be based upon the *Pathauto* patterns specified by the administrator at *Administration>Configuration>Search and Metadata>URL aliases*. In Drupal 6 the same feature is located at *Administration>Site Building>URL aliases*.

The *Pathauto* module comes with several default patterns that provide automatic aliases for the different types of content, such as vocabularies, taxonomy terms, menus, nodes, users, user blogs (list of blog posts), and core content types such as story, page, book.

3.4   User management

Typically, users register on a site and an email is sent asking them to verify their email address and login to the site. However, the site administrator may want to control this process differently. Therefore, other options to add and manage new users are available on the *People* page; *Administration>People* or http://mysite.com/admin/people. You may mange user roles and permissions by clicking on the *Permissions* tab on this page. To change the process by which users apply for accounts, visit the *People and Permissions page (Administration>Configuration>People: Account settings)* or http://mysite.com/admin/config/people/accounts.

3.4.1   Registration and login

Unless you have resolved to do an unwise thing such as giving the entire world unlimited access to all parts of your web site, or you need to use it only as a personal blog to which only you may contribute articles, you will want to limit access to some features to only registered users. On a new Drupal site, you will find the registration and login form in a side bar. You can remove this block altogether, or relocate it to any other block area of the site on the *Blocks* administration page. Rules for registration of users can be set in the *Administration* panel.

3.4.2 Open ID

Typically, a registered user will log in by using a username and password they specify or a site generated username and password. If you have opened your site up to the API of social media applications such as Twitter or Facebook, the user may be able to complete their registration and log in by using the links generated by these third party applications. Internally however, Drupal permits login through the *OpenID* interface which is provided by the *OpenID* module. If this module is enabled, it will add a new link to the *User login* block, and this link will allow a user to sign in using *OpenID* (Figure 3.20).

Figure 3.20   Using the OpenID login

OpenID is a secure method, which permits logging into many websites by using a single username and password. The basic concept of OpenID is as follows:

■   A user has an account on an OpenID server which provides a unique URL (such as myusername.openidprovider.com).

- When the user comes to a site, which supports the OpenID login, they are presented with the option of entering this URL.
- The site now communicates with the OpenID server, asking it to verify the identity of the user.
- If the user is logged into their OpenID server, the server communicates back to the site, verifying the user. If they are not logged in, the OpenID server will ask the user for their password.

OpenID works in the same way as enabling the site to automatically register and login new users via their Twitter or Facebook accounts.

3.5   Backing up and restoring a Drupal Site

When you back up a site, you are creating copies of both the files and the database. Backing up can protect against a disaster, arising from a database crash or hostile attack on the web site. A backup can assist in recovering the site if necessary. There are several ways to do a backup, depending on the administrator's preference or level of technical ability. The following sections provide options for backing up and restoring a Drupal site.

3.5.1   Backing up a Drupal site using a GUI

This is a fairly easy process and the decision to use this method, may depend on the size of the site. For example, backing up a site with a large database and gigabytes of files may prove quite time-consuming using this method. However, with a small site it may be effective.

3.5.1.1   Backup a Drupal site using a graphical FTP client

A graphical FTP client such as FileZilla, can be used to download all your existing Drupal files to a folder on your hard drive. If your Internet connection speed is good, this shouldn't take more than a few minutes.

3.5.1.2   Backup your database with PhpMyAdmin

To access phpMyAdmin you need to login into your hosting account control panel. After getting to the phpMyAdmin page, select your database, click the *Export* tab, and then click *select all*.

Be sure to check the *structure* and *data* checkboxes. Finally, check the *Save as File* checkbox and then click on the *Go* button to save the .sql file to your desktop. For peace of mind, and to make the file easy to find later, it may be wise to put this .sql file in the same folder where you backed up the other Drupal files.

3.5.2   Backing up a Drupal site using the command line

If you have shell access to your server, you can copy the contents of your Drupal directory as well as the database to a directory outside the website.

3.5.2.1   Backup files to a directory using the command line

The following command will copy all the files, together with the .htaccess file from your Drupal directory to the backup directory:

```
cp -rp /path/to/drupal_site/path/to/backup_dir
```

The -rp option indicates copy recursive and preserve permissions.

3.5.2.2   Files backup to a compressed archive using the command

Alternatively, you can archive and compress all the files, together with the .htaccess file from the Drupal directory to the backup directory. To do this, change to the Drupal directory and execute the following:

```
tar czf drupalbackup.tgz /path/to/drupal_site/
```

To verify this worked, extract the files into a new directory with the following command:

```
tar xzf drupalbackup.tgz
```

3.5.3   Backing up a Drupal database using the command line

There are several methods to backup a Drupal database. You could use the *Backup and Migrate* module, a nifty tool that makes the process easy. You could similarly use *Drush*, which is a Drupal command line tool. Administrators that are more skilled may prefer to use SQL dump scripts. For example the following MySQL dump command creates a copy of the database:

```
mysqldump -u USERNAME -p DATABASENAME>/path/to/backup_dir/
database-backup.sql
```

In addition, the following Drush command (*sql-dump*) creates a copy of the database. From the Drupal directory execute this command:

```
drush sql-dump result-file=/path/to/backup_dir/database-
backup.sql
```

For more information on how to use Drush go to the Drupal web site.

3.5.4   Restoring a database backup using command line

Before doing a database restoration, it may be wise to empty the destination database in order to prevent errors from arising due to conflicts between the local tables and the destination tables.

The easiest way to empty the tables is to simply drop the entire database and create a new one. If you have CREATE DATABASE privileges at the shell, then the simplest way to do this is as follows:

```
mysql -h HOST -u USERNAME -p PASSWORD
drop database `DB_NAME`;
create database `DB_NAME` charset utf8;
quit
```

However, if you on a shared hosting site and you do not have CREATE DATABASE privileges at the shell, you need to access PHPMyAdmin through your hosting account Control Panel and manually delete all the tables before restoring the database dump.

3.5.4.1   Restoring a Drupal database from a MySQL dump using the command line

After all the tables in your database have been dropped, you can restore your database backup using the following command:

```
mysql -h HOST -u USERNAME -p PASSWORD < your-db-dump.sql
```

3.6   Migrating a Drupal site (server to server)

Usually, you would have built your site in a development environment such as on a local machine and need to later move to a live server.

The need may arise to move a site from one server to another. This is a fairly simple process, but there are problems to watch out for else the migration may fail. Before you start, you must be sure the two server environments are identical. In particular, document any differences in the PHP, MySQL and Apache installation on the two servers—especially bugs, features, modules, configurations and versions. You must also ensure that the target server supports the *mod_rewrite, AllowOverride* features that Drupal requires.

We have covered how to backup and restore databases and files, but let's look at the *migration* process in a systematic way.

3.6.1   Steps in migrating a Drupal site

Step 1.   Document the modules that are used on the old site, especially their versions, paths etc. The contributed module Site Documentation can ease this task.

Step 2.   Document the temporary directory folder that is used in the admin/settings/file of the old site. This must be replicated in the new site, else Drupal may find it impossible to locate some files.

Step 3.   Set the site to maintenance mode. Go to the *Administration>Site maintenance* page and set it to *Off line*.

Step 4.   If the *Status reports* page shows that the Drupal scripts are obsolete, consider updating the Drupal core and modules before proceeding with the migration. However, you may choose to do this on the new site.

Step 5.   Turn off clean URLs. On the new site you will temporarily have to access the administrator page through www.newsite.com/?q=user. This will give you the login form.

Step 6.   Clear the cache tables. The cache data usually causes confusion especially with URL paths. The *devel* module and *admin menu* module contain tools to do this. You may otherwise visit www.mysite.com/admin/settings/performance and click the Clear cached data button at the bottom of the page.

Step 7.   Export your database. You can use phpMyAdmin for this, and it should produce a text file with a .sql extension, which will be downloaded to your local computer.

Step 8.   Copy all site files including Drupal files, modules, and themes and put them on the new server. You could choose to use fresh files from the Drupal repository instead of copying from your local machine.

Step 9.   Copy the files directory and any similar directories such as image galleries, which Drupal has created during installation, and transfer them directly to the new server.

Step 10.   And finally, if you are moving a live site from one server to another you will definitely need to adjust the DNS settings to point to the new server.

3.6.2   Restoring a site

To restore your site to a new server, simply upload the SQL backup to the database, and all things being equal, the new site should work the same as the old site. Several Drupal tools that can help ensure this process is done correctly. For instance, there are modules such as *Backup and Migrate*, which will assist you in backing up and restoring your data. Used in tandem with some related modules such as *Backup and Migrate Files*, it will also backup all site files.

3.7   Performance and security

Security, performance, user interaction, maintenance, and quality assurance are the real issues a live site will have to contend with on a daily basis. Failure to address these matters could lead to disaster. However, it is not a daunting task to stay on top of these issues.

3.7.1   Performance

A live site, especially working with many installed modules or with heavy traffic could begin to run slowly and frustrate the users. Much of this problem can be alleviated by implementing Drupal's built-in *caching* and *bandwidth optimization* mechanisms. With caching, highly requested pages are stored in a cache for ready access without making demands on the database. If scripts like CSS and JavaScript are aggregated, pages will load faster because the scripts for the individual elements on the page will not have to be loaded separately.

To implement caching and aggregation, go to the Configuration>Performance page (Figure 3.21) or http://mysite.com/admin/config/development/performance link and enable the following:

- Cache pages for anonymous users
- Cache blocks
- Aggregate and compress CSS files
- Aggregate JavaScript files

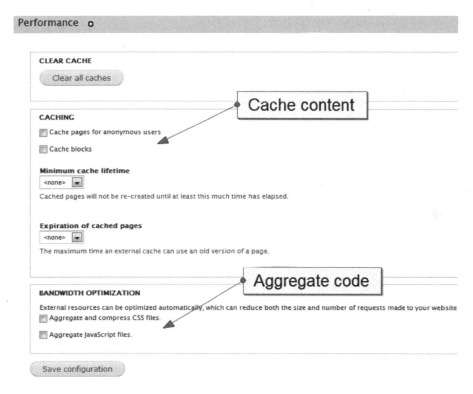

Figure 3.21   Performance administration page

3.7.2   User interaction

Even if your site is of minor interest, but you have opened it up for other users to post their content, spammers will eventually find it. Therefore, it may be important to learn how to make contingency plans to protect your site forms, including the content posting forms against spam attack.

The more common methods of protection are to install and enable CAPTCHA, reCAPTCHA, or an anti-spam service such as *Mollom*. Spammers begin their journey into a Drupal site by giving false emails during registration. It is wise to ensure users are verified through their email, even though this is becoming less effective as other means of protection. reCAPTCHA is a great tool and will frustrate most spammers, but it may also frustrate well-intentioned users who may not understand why it is so difficult for them to post content.

3.7.3   Security

Drupal scripts are regularly reviewed for security and usability. The same applies to most of the contributed modules and themes. However, no script is ever infallible and it is a good practice to take steps to make sure that your Drupal site is safe from *planned accidents*. The following suggestions should help.

■ Always make it a habit to check *Reports>Status report* and make sure there are no warnings or errors.
■ On the *User Settings* page, verify that account creation settings are as you intend. For example, if you have permitted users to create their own accounts do they need approval? If so, make sure the settings take cognizance of this aspect of your registration process.
■ Always regularly upgrade the Drupal Core and Contributed modules to the latest version to ensure that security loopholes are constantly patched.
■ On the *Permissions page*, verify what permissions anonymous and authenticated users have been given. It is not rare to find that an administrator has inadvertently given anonymous users permission to administer their site!
■ Are your admin passwords secure? Use complex passwords that cannot be easily guessed.
■ Sometimes when there are site errors, PHP code is generated on top of pages and can be visible to all users. These error reports can reveal information that can be used by hackers to exploit your site. It is often a good idea in a live site to turn off on-screen error reporting. Do this at *Administration>Settings>error-reporting*.

3.8   Summary

This chapter gives an overview of the administrative tools available on a Drupal site. It briefly explains the administrative features and how to use them to ensure that your site works optimally. The chapter also shows how to backup a Drupal site and how to migrate it from one server to another. Finally, the chapter addresses security and performance issues that a live site will have to contend with on a daily basis with hints on how to prevent them.

Chapter 4

Creating Drupal Themes

In the previous chapter, we discussed the essentials of administering a Drupal site. The chapter briefly examined the primary Drupal functionality and explains how to configure them. We also learned how to backup a Drupal site, how to migrate a site from one server to another and about security and performance issues. In this chapter we will look at how to create a unique look and feel for a Drupal site by building a new theme from scratch.

Experienced users of Drupal will argue that to create a new theme it is better to take a contributed them and modify. Even though this may save time and minimize the possibility of the occurrence of coding errors, it may be a problem later especially when the master theme becomes incompatible with a new Drupal version. This chapter is important because of the following reasons:

- It will enable the user to build a non-generic theme.
- It will enable the user to understand how a Drupal theme structure works. Including what files are necessary and what files are expendable.
- It will show the user how to create custom PHPTemplate files.
- It will show the user how to customize a theme's appearance with Cascading Style Sheets (CSS).

This chapter will examine and refer to contributed themes. This is done to show practical examples of the structure of the individual files that are typically found in theme folders.

4.1 How a theme works

The objective of a Drupal theme is to separate the processing logic of the framework from the design element. For this, Drupal employs a complex

69

theme system, which consists of themes, theme engines and hooks. This theme system works together with the Drupal core and the module design elements to create a distinctive look and feel for the user interface.

The primary motivation for the separation of Drupal business logic from its presentation logic are as follows:

1.   It makes the code easier to maintain.

2.   It makes it possible to swap out the implementation of the theme layer without having to rewrite the code layer and vise-versa.

The basic architecture of the Drupal framework is shown in Figure 4.1. Themes are used to display data, fetched from the database by the Drupal core, through an underlying *Theme Engine* which acts as an interface between the Drupal core and the theme templates.

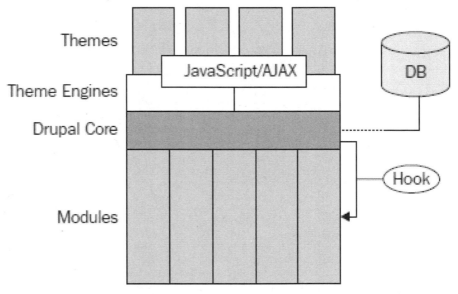

Figure 4.1   The Drupal schema

In the Drupal theme system, each piece of content is handled separately as it's passed through this system. This means that each elemental body of data is individually themed before being combined into larger bodies of data, which are again themed. The aggregation process goes on until the combined data bodies are ready to be displayed in the browser. (Figure 4.2).

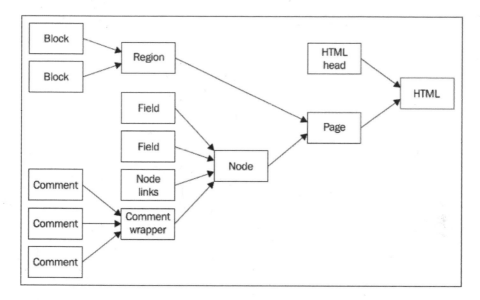

Figure 4.2   The Drupal theme schema

As an example, when comments for a typical node are extracted from the database, they pass through the theme system where HTML markup is added at each layer. The *comment wrapper* aggregates the comments together and adds additional markup and a *new comment* form. This wrapper is then passed to the node layer where it is again combined with other pieces of the node's original content. This process is repeated until the entire HTML page is completely built and becomes ready to be sent to a web browser.

The advantage of this granularity is that theme developers can be as imaginative as they want when creating theme markup.

4.1.1   Theme Engines

Theme engines are the means through which themes interact with Drupal core. Several theme engines may be used with Drupal. The following are popular, but theme developers may actually use their own custom engine if they wish.

4.1.1.1   PHPTemplate theme engine

This engine uses individual theme files with names like filename.tpl.php files to theme Drupal's theme_filename() functions. Each of these files contains an HTML skeleton and some PHP statements for the dynamic data.

Thus, with a basic knowledge of PHP, it is not difficult to create advanced themes with PHPTemplate since only small bits of code are involved.

4.1.1.2   Template theme engine

This theme system also does the layout and styles for the web page by means of templates. The system completely separates logic (PHP), structure (XHTML/HTML), and style (CSS). Thus, the designers may create or modify templates by working on CSS and XHTML/HTML without having to worry about any PHP coding.

4.1.1.3   Plain PHP themes

This system directly themes Drupal through overrides for Drupal's built-in theme functions. The theme will override the basic theme hooks such as pages, nodes, blocks, but any other element can be similarly themed. The contributed Chameleon theme is an example.

4.1.1.4   The Smarty theme engine

Similar to PHPTemplate, this theme engine uses individual filename.tpl files to theme Drupal's theme_filename() functions. Note though that in this case the extension is .tpl and not .tpl.php. Also, for the PHPTEmplate engine, every template file contains an HTML skeleton with Smarty tags for the dynamic data.

There are several other theme engines commonly used with Drupal including PHPTAL, wgSmarty, Zengine, Awesomengine, ETS, Haml, XSLengine and Peroxide. In this book we will be using the PHPTemplate engine because it is the default theme engine packaged with Drupal 7. It also has no external dependencies and needs no external configuration outside of the Drupal framework. More than 99% of contributed themes in the Drupal repository use the PHPTemplate theme engine.

4.1.2   Theme hooks

Hooks are the mechanism which facilitate interaction between the layers of Drupal. Themes and theme engines specifically implement hooks for purposes such as handling a particular request for display, especially from a module. In interactions within the Drupal core, template files also behave in a similar way as hooks. Thus, in the same way as Drupal searches for hook functions to implement the functionality of a module, it may also search for template files which follow a certain naming convention and load those files to create a display. Theme hooks are more relevant to interaction of the theme with modules and will not be discussed in any detail in this chapter.

4.2   Planning a theme

A theme is made up of a number of files. How many of them will depend on the complexity of the theme. A theme can have as few as three files or it can have several dozen files including graphic elements and various scripts placed in folders within the theme directory. The following illustrates the typical file descriptions that you may expect to find within the main folder of a theme (Figure 4.3).

Name	Date modified	Type	Size
color	11/15/2011 2:12 PM	File Folder	
images	11/15/2011 2:12 PM	File Folder	
comment.tpl	12/1/2010 12:18 AM	PHP File	1 KB
fix-ie	4/28/2010 8:08 PM	Cascading Style S...	2 KB
fix-ie-rtl	4/28/2010 8:08 PM	Cascading Style S...	2 KB
garland	1/5/2011 6:25 AM	INFO File	1 KB
logo	6/29/2010 3:39 PM	PNG Image	5 KB
maintenance-page.tpl	3/4/2010 9:03 AM	PHP File	3 KB
node.tpl	12/1/2010 12:18 AM	PHP File	2 KB
page.tpl	11/20/2010 4:03 AM	PHP File	3 KB
print	4/28/2010 8:08 PM	Cascading Style S...	2 KB
screenshot	6/29/2010 3:39 PM	PNG Image	11 KB
style	1/3/2011 7:04 AM	Cascading Style S...	21 KB
style-rtl	9/27/2010 1:12 AM	Cascading Style S...	5 KB
template	12/1/2010 12:18 AM	PHP File	5 KB
theme-settings	9/4/2010 3:21 PM	PHP File	1 KB

Figure 4.3   Structure of a typical Drupal theme

The figure above represents a lot of files and brings up the prospect of the work ahead for the new theme builder. But, as we shall learn in the following sections not all these files are necessary in a theme, and some themes don't even have a CSS file. However, what the directory should show is that different regions and functions of a theme page are often controlled by different templates–and this is the desirable scenario.

In the diagram below(Figure 4.4), we will learn how various Drupal theme templates are used in composing the typical page view. The

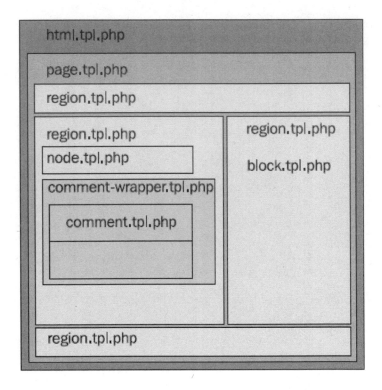

Figure 4.4   The typical theme files and how they interact

region.tpl.php file is called up for a region, such as the footer if a corresponding file exists, and if not the default theme file is used.

Understanding how these theme files are used should be able to give educated hints on the structure of a theme and how it works. Let's look at some of the files in the theme directory and examine their functionality within the overall theme.

4.2.1   The .info file

This file is required. It must be included for Drupal to call a theme. The .info files tell Drupal the internal name of the theme. For example, if this file is named *example.info*, then Drupal will call the theme *example*. This naming convention is specific to Drupal 7 and Drupal 6 themes. Earlier releases will employ the name of the enclosing folder of the theme, rather than the .info file.

Also, if the theme uses elements as JavaScript, metadata, stylesheets, or block regions, then it should be defined inside the .info file. Everything else is optional. Below is the content of the .info file for the Bartik theme .

```
; $Id: bartik.info,v 1.5 2010/11/07 00:27:20 dries Exp $

name = Bartik
description = A flexible, recolorable theme with many regions.
package = Core
version = VERSION
core = 7.x

stylesheets[all][] = css/layout.css
stylesheets[all][] = css/style.css
stylesheets[all][] = css/colors.css
stylesheets[print][] = css/print.css

regions[header] = Header
regions[help] = Help
regions[page_top] = Page top
regions[page_bottom] = Page bottom
regions[highlighted] = Highlighted

regions[featured] = Featured
regions[content] = Content
regions[sidebar_first] = Sidebar first
regions[sidebar_second] = Sidebar second

regions[triptych_first] = Triptych first
regions[triptych_middle] = Triptych middle
regions[triptych_last] = Triptych last

regions[footer_firstcolumn] = Footer first column
regions[footer_secondcolumn] = Footer second column
regions[footer_thirdcolumn] = Footer third column
regions[footer_fourthcolumn] = Footer fourth column
regions[footer] = Footer

settings[shortcut_module_link] = 0

; Information added by drupal.org packaging script on 2011-01-05
version = "7.0"
project = "drupal"
datestamp = "1294208756"
```

4.2.2   The .tpl.php template files

The theme directory will contain several template files with names such as xxx.tpl.php. These template files are used for the *(x)*HTML markup and PHP variables of the theme. In some situations, they may be coded to output other types of data such as RSS feeds.

Generally speaking, each .tpl.php file is coded to handle specific data outputs. This is because it may be confusing and counterproductive to embed complex logic in template files because they can become difficult to maintain. It is desirable to have them contain nothing more than straight *(x)*HTML tags and PHP variables.

In some cases, one template file may be coded to handle multiple .tpl.php files through *suggestions*. Template suggestions are alternate templates based on an existing file, which are used when a specific condition is met and a file that matches the suggestion exists. The suggestions are always optional, and if no such file exists in the theme it will fall back to the default output. For more information on how template suggestions work, see http://drupal.org/node/223440.

The code below describes the content of the node.tpl.php file which describes the output of the basic node for the core Garland theme.

```php
<?php
// $Id: node.tpl.php,v 1.24 2010/12/01 00:18:15 webchick Exp $
?>
<div id="node-<?php print $node->nid; ?>" class="<?php print
$classes; ?>"<?php print $attributes; ?>>

  <?php print $user_picture; ?>

  <?php print render($title_prefix); ?>
  <?php if (!$page): ?>
    <h2<?php print $title_attributes; ?>><a href="<?php print
$node_url; ?>"><?php print $title; ?></a></h2>
  <?php endif; ?>
  <?php print render($title_suffix); ?>

  <?php if ($display_submitted): ?>
    <span class="submitted"><?php print $submitted ?></span>
  <?php endif; ?>
```

```
<div class="content clearfix"<?php print $content_attributes;
?>>
    <?php
    // We hide the comments and links now so that we can render
them later.
        hide($content['comments']);
        hide($content['links']);
        print render($content);
    ?>
  </div>

  <div class="clearfix">
    <?php if (!empty($content['links'])): ?>
      <div class="links"><?php print render($content['links']);
?></div>
    <?php endif; ?>

    <?php print render($content['comments']); ?>
  </div>

</div>
```

4.2.3   The template.php file

The template.php file typically holds all the conditional logic and data processing for the output of the theme. The template.php file may be used to keep the .tpl.php files for the theme tidy. It may incorporate preprocessors for generating variables to be merged with the markup inside .tpl.php files. Therefore, in a complex theme, the template.php file may improve maintainability.

The template.php file could include custom functions, as well as overriding theme functions and any other customization required by the raw output. Since it is a PHP file, the content must start with a PHP opening tag "<?php", but it is often recommended to omit the close tag. The following extract from the template.php file of the core Garland theme should illustrate what a file of this type typically contains:

```
<?php
// $Id: template.php,v 1.45 2010/12/01 00:18:15 webchick Exp $

/**
 * Return a themed breadcrumb trail.
```

```
  *
  * @param $breadcrumb
  *   An array containing the breadcrumb links.
  * @return a string containing the breadcrumb output.
  */
function garland_breadcrumb($variables) {
  $breadcrumb = $variables['breadcrumb'];

  if (!empty($breadcrumb)) {
    // Provide a navigational heading to give context for
breadcrumb links to
    // screen-reader users. Make the heading invisible with
.element-invisible.
    $output = '<h2 class="element-invisible">' . t('You are
here') . '</h2>';

    $output .= '<div class="breadcrumb">' . implode(' â€º ',
$breadcrumb) . '</div>';
    return $output;
  }
}


/**
 * Override or insert variables into the maintenance page
template.
 */
function garland_preprocess_maintenance_page(&$vars) {
  // While markup for normal pages is split into
page.tpl.php and html.tpl.php,
  // the markup for the maintenance page is all in the single
  // maintenance-page.tpl.php template. So, to have what's done
in
  // garland_preprocess_html() also happen on the maintenance
page, it has to be
  // called here.
  garland_preprocess_html($vars);
}


/**
 * Override or insert variables into the html template.
 */
function garland_preprocess_html(&$vars) {
  // Toggle fixed or fluid width.
```

```
  if (theme_get_setting('garland_width') == 'fluid') {
    $vars['classes_array'][] = 'fluid-width';
  }
  // Add conditional CSS for IE6.
  drupal_add_css(path_to_theme() . '/fix-ie.css', array('group'
=> CSS_THEME, 'browsers' => array('IE' => 'lt IE 7', '!IE' =>
FALSE), 'preprocess' => FALSE));
}

/**
 * Override or insert variables into the html template.
 */
function garland_process_html(&$vars) {
  // Hook into color.module
  if (module_exists('color')) {
    _color_html_alter($vars);
  }
}
```

4.2.4   Sub-themes

Sub-themes are derived from a parent theme and inherit the resources from the parent theme. To create a sub-theme, a base theme entry inside the .info file is needed. From there it will inherit the resources from its parent theme.

4.2.5   Others

There are several other elements that you may find in themes, and may not be required for the theme to function. These include logo and screenshot, the theme-settings.php and the color.inc files.

4.2.5.1   The logo and screenshot elements

These are not necessary for the theme to function, but they are recommended. If for example you will wish to contribute your theme to the Drupal repository, a screenshot may be mandatory. The screenshots will typically be found on the theme administration page and in the user account settings for selecting themes. Following (Figure 4.5) is screenshot for the Garland theme.

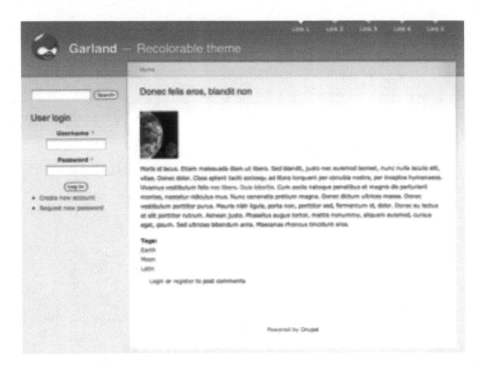

Figure 4.5   Garland theme screenshot

4.2.5.2   The theme-settings.php file

This file is used to supply administrative UI settings or advanced features beyond the general settings which include logo, search, mission, etc.. A look at the content of this file for the Garland theme should show an indication of what it will eventually display:

```php
<?php
// $Id: theme-settings.php,v 1.3 2010/09/04 15:21:09 dries Exp $

/**
 * @file
 * Theme setting callbacks for the garland theme.
 */

/**
 * Implements hook_form_FORM_ID_alter().
 *
 * @param $form
 *   The form.
```

```
 * @param $form_state
 *    The form state.
 */
function garland_form_system_theme_settings_alter(&$form,
&$form_state) {

  $form['garland_width'] = array(
    '#type' => 'radios',
    '#title' => t('Content width'),
    '#options' => array(
      'fluid' => t('Fluid width'),
      'fixed' => t('Fixed width'),
    ),
    '#default_value' => theme_get_setting('garland_width'),
    '#description' => t('Specify whether the content will wrap
to a fixed width or will fluidly expand to the width of the
browser window.'),
    // Place this above the color scheme options.
    '#weight' => -2,
  );
}
```

The eventual display (Figure 4.6) will be a form which looks like the following.

Figure 4.6   The settings page also showing color setting

4.2.5.3   The color.inc file

The color module allows administrators to completely change the color scheme of a theme without having to manually work on the stylesheets. The color module can alter the stylesheet and re-render images. However, the design of the theme must be able to accommodate this, and must also provide specific theme hooks to allow this.

If your theme requires color module support, a *color* directory, then a color.inc file is needed along with other support files. Otherwise, you may omit it.

4.3   Building the theme

There are three basic methods to build a theme in order of difficulty:

1.   Build from scratch

2.   Use a tool such as the Theme builder module

3.   Modify an existing theme

We will assume, for reasons previously mentioned, that we will not be altering another theme, but building a new theme from scratch. However, all along the way we will keep the contents of some existing themes handy to see what the structure looks like.

4.3.1   Creating the directory structure

First, you need to create a directory to contain the theme files. The desirable place to put this directory will be in the sites/all/themes directory. The directory should be given a unique name that describes your theme, and this name should have no spaces.

Although not required, it may be helpful to create sub-directories for images, CSS files, and scripts if your theme uses them. This helps to keep things organized. A directory structure for a simple theme could look like this:

- Theme name
    - css
    - images
    - scripts

4.3.2 Building the info file

The .info file is a static text file with the parameters needed to describe the structure as well as the content and configuration of the theme. Inside this text file, each of the lines is a key-value pair with the key on the the left and the value on the right of an equals sign. Example:

```
; $Id: garland.info,v 1.10 2010/11/07 00:27:20 dries Exp $
name = Garland
description = A multi-column theme which can be configured to
modify colors and switch between fixed and fluid width layouts.
package = Core
version = VERSION
core = 7.x
stylesheets[all][] = style.css
stylesheets[print][] = print.css
settings[garland_width] = fluid

; Information added by drupal.org packaging script on 2011-01-05
version = "7.0"
project = "drupal"
```

Semicolons are used on the left to add comments. Square brackets are used for building a list of associated values, referred to as an array. If specific required keys are not present in the .info file, Drupal will utilize default values.

4.3.2.1 Name

This is a required value. It should be a human readable name and must start with an alphabetic character. The name has the same limitation for creating functions in PHP because it is also used by Drupal in the same way. This means that, like for all PHP functions. the name may contain numbers and underscores, but may not contain hyphens, spaces or punctuation.

Components installed in Drupal should have unique names. For example, it is unwise to use a name used by a module for the theme name. If this proves difficult, append a prefix that is likely to be unique for naming the theme. Therefore if the name of the site is *model.com*, consider naming your theme *model_themename*.

Syntax:

```
name = Garland
```

4.3.2.2   Description

This key is not required, but recommended and should be a short description of the theme. This description will be displayed on the *theme selection* or *Appearance* page.

Syntax:

> description = A multi-column theme which can be configured to modify colors and switch between fixed and fluid width layouts.

4.3.2.3   Screenshot

This key is optional. Its function is to tell Drupal where to find the thumbnail image of the theme. The thumbnail image is used on the theme selection page. If this key is not written into the .info file, Drupal will call up the default screenshot.png file in the theme's directory.

If the thumbnail file is not called screenshot.png or if you want to place the screenshot file in another directory outside of the theme's main directory, include this key.

Syntax:

```
screenshot = /images/screenshot.png
```

4.3.2.4   Version

Even though many of the popular themes include this key, it is discouraged. If you intend to contribute the theme in the Drupal themes repository, the version string will be automatically added by drupal.org when a release is created and packaged. If your theme is not being hosted on the drupal.org web site, you can safely include whatever version string that matches your requirements.

Syntax:

```
version = 1.0
```

4.3.2.5   Core

This is a required value. In all presently supported Drupal versions, all .info files for *modules and themes* **are required to indicate** the major version of the Drupal core with which they are compatible. If the value set here is compared with the *DRUPAL_CORE_COMPATIBILITY* constant (found in the include/bootstrap.inc file) and no match is found, the *theme will be disabled by Drupal.*

```php
<?php
define('DRUPAL_CORE_COMPATIBILITY', '7.x')
?>
```

If you are contributing your theme, the drupal.org packaging script automatically sets this value based on the Drupal core compatibility setting for each release node. In which case users downloading the packaged themes from drupal.org will always be sure they are getting the theme version compatible with their Drupal version. If however, you deploy Drupal directly from git, it can help to commit all changes to the .info file for your theme to indicate to users what version of core the HEAD of git is compatible with at any given time.

Syntax:

```
core = 7.x
```

4.3.2.6   Engine

This indicates the theme engine used by the theme. It is required in most cases. If none is supplied in the .info file, Drupal assumes that the theme is standalone, which is implemented with a .theme file. Most of the themes found in the Drupal.org repository use the PHPTemplate default engine, and which is packaged with the Drupal core.

Syntax:

```
engine = phptemplate
```

4.3.2.7   Base theme

If the theme is a sub-theme to another theme, then it should declare its base theme in order to enable theme inheritance—which means the resources from the base theme will cascade from and be reused inside the sub-theme. Use the internal *machine* readable name of the base theme.

Syntax:

```
base theme = garland
```

4.3.2.8   Regions

This defines the block regions available to the theme. You will need to specify the key of regions followed by the internal *machine* readable name in square brackets and the human readable name as the value. If no regions are defined, the following values are assumed for Drupal 7 themes.

```
regions[header] = Header
regions[highlighted] = Highlighted
regions[help] = Help
regions[content] = Content
regions[sidebar_first] = Left sidebar
regions[sidebar_second] = Right sidebar
regions[footer] = Footer
```

These values may be overridden for your specific needs. If you have done that, you must declare the line.

Syntax:

```
regions[highlighted] = Mission Statement
```

4.3.2.9   Features

Various page elements output by the theme can be toggled on and off on the theme's configuration page. The *features* keys control which of these check boxes are displayed on the theme's configuration page. This is useful for suppressing check boxes for elements not defined or used by a theme. To suppress a check box, omit the entry for it. However, if none are defined, all the check boxes will be displayed by default.

The example below (Figure 4.7) lists all the available elements controlled by the features key.

```
features[ ] = logo
features[ ] = name
features[ ] = slogan
features[ ] = node_user_picture
features[ ] = comment_user_picture
features[ ] = favicon
features[ ] = main_menu
features[ ] = secondary_menu
```

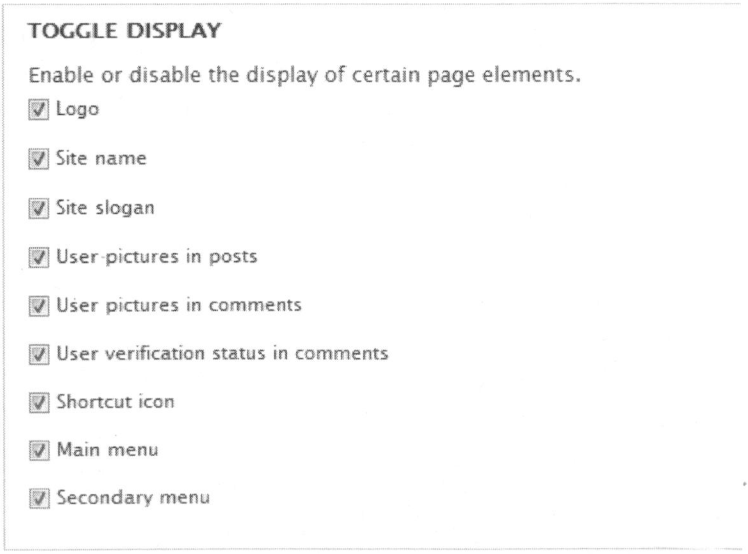

TOGGLE DISPLAY

Enable or disable the display of certain page elements.

☑ Logo

☑ Site name

☑ Site slogan

☑ User pictures in posts

☑ User pictures in comments

☑ User verification status in comments

☑ Shortcut icon

☑ Main menu

☑ Secondary menu

Figure 4.7   Theme features administration

4.3.2.10   Stylesheets

In previous versions, Drupal themes automatically default to settings contained in style.css. Additional stylesheets can also be added by calling drupal_add_css() in the template.php file of the theme. However, in current versions, themes no longer default to using style.css, if it is not specified in the .info file. New stylesheets can also be added through the .info file.

Syntax:

```
stylesheets[all][] = css/style.css
stylesheets[print][] = css/print.css
```

4.3.2.11   Scripts

In previous versions, it was common for themes to add Javascript by calling function drupal_add_js() in the template.php file. However, in Drupal 7, script.js is only included if it has been specified in the .info file.

Syntax:

```
scripts[] = scripts/myscript.js
```

4.3.2.12   PHP

This string defines the minimum PHP version which the theme supports. The default value is derived from the *DRUPAL_MINIMUM_PHP* constant, (located in the *includes/bootstrap.inc* file) and defines the minimum required version for the rest of core.

```
<?php
define('DRUPAL_MINIMUM_PHP', '5.2.4')
?>
```

This value can be changed to another version if desired, but adding the string is not required.

Syntax:

```
php = 5.2.4
```

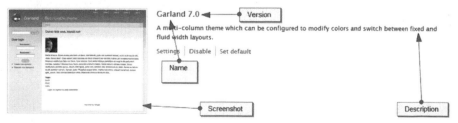

Figure 4.8   The theme description page

4.3.2.13　Example .info file

What does Drupal do with the information that you have supplied in the .info file? In summary, the values are applied on the selection page, the configuration pages, and as instructions to the core on where to find essential files (Figure 4.8).

```
name = Garland
description = A multi-column theme which can be configured to
modify colors and switch between fixed and fluid width layouts.
package = Core
version = VERSION
core = 7.x
stylesheets[all][] = style.css
stylesheets[print][] = print.css
settings[garland_width] = fluid


; Information added by drupal.org packaging script on 2011-01-05
version = "7.0"
project = "drupal"
datestamp = "1294208756"
```

Note that everything from the line "; Information added by drupal.org packaging script on 2011-01-05" and down is added by the drupal.org packaging script. The project and datestamp keys should never be manually added.

4.3.2.14　Default .info values

There are default values that are always assumed by Drupal for every installed theme. If these values are not defined in the .info file, the theme will automatically use these default values.

However, these default values apply as a group. This means that if you override a region with regions[sub_header] = Sub-header, the rest of the default regions will be omitted unless they are redefined in the .info file. This also applies to stylesheets. When another stylesheet is defined, this will prevent style.css from being included unless it is also redefined.

The following keys and values are the defaults for a Drupal 7 theme.

Regions

```
regions[sidebar_first]  = Left sidebar
regions[sidebar_second] = Right sidebar
regions[content] = Content
regions[header] = Header
regions[footer] = Footer
regions[highlighted] = Highlighted
regions[help] = Help
regions[page_top] = Page Top
regions[page_bottom] = Page Bottom
```

Engine

```
engine = phptemplate
```

Features

```
features[ ] = logo
features[ ] = name
features[ ] = slogan
features[ ] = node_user_picture
features[ ] = comment_user_picture
features[ ] = favicon
features[ ] = main_menu
features[ ] = secondary_menu
```

Screenshot

```
screenshot = screenshot.png
```

4.3.3   Building the page.tpl.php file

As a start let us look at the content of a typical page.tpl.php file (Figure 4.9). This one is from the Garland theme and shows what the source code looks like in a browser.

Figure 4.9   Content of a typical page.tpl.file in a browser

At first glance, the page.tpl.php file looks very complex. However, upcon closer examination, it is just a simple HTML marked up page with a PHP statements added in. Conveniently, most of the PHP elements have already been defined for Drupal and all you need to do is place them as you wish.

The link http://drupal.org/node/190815 (Core Templates) will display a page.tpl.php link which will take you to the following list of variables for the page.tpl.php template (Figure 4.10).

page.tpl.php

Drupal 6   **Drupal 7**
View documentation   View source

Default theme implementation to display a single Drupal page.

Available variables:

General utility variables:

- $base_path: The base URL path of the Drupal installation. At the very least, this will always default to /.
- $directory: The directory the template is located in, e.g. modules/system or themes/bartik.
- $is_front: TRUE if the current page is the front page.
- $logged_in: TRUE if the user is registered and signed in.
- $is_admin: TRUE if the user has permission to access administration pages.

Site identity:

- $front_page: The URL of the front page. Use this instead of $base_path, when linking to the front page. This includes the language domain or prefix.
- $logo: The path to the logo image, as defined in theme configuration.
- $site_name: The name of the site, empty when display has been disabled in theme settings.
- $site_slogan: The slogan of the site, empty when display has been disabled in theme settings.

Navigation:

- $main_menu (array): An array containing the Main menu links for the site, if they have been configured.
- $secondary_menu (array): An array containing the Secondary menu links for the site, if they have been configured.
- $breadcrumb: The breadcrumb trail for the current page.

Page content (in order of occurrence in the default page.tpl.php):

- $title_prefix (array): An array containing additional output populated by modules, intended to be displayed in front of the main title tag that appears in the template.
- $title: The page title, for use in the actual HTML content.
- $title_suffix (array): An array containing additional output populated by modules, intended to be displayed after the main title tag that appears in the template.
- $messages: HTML for status and error messages. Should be displayed prominently.
- $tabs (array): Tabs linking to any sub-pages beneath the current page (e.g., the view and edit tabs when displaying a node).
- $action_links (array): Actions local to the page, such as 'Add menu' on the menu administration interface.
- $feed_icons: A string of all feed icons for the current page.
- $node: The node object, if there is an automatically-loaded node associated with the page, and the node ID is the second argument in the page's path (e.g. node/12345 and node/12345/revisions, but not comment/reply/12345).

Regions:

- $page['help']: Dynamic help text, mostly for admin pages.
- $page['highlighted']: Items for the highlighted content region.
- $page['content']: The main content of the current page.
- $page['sidebar_first']: Items for the first sidebar.
- $page['sidebar_second']: Items for the second sidebar.
- $page['header']: Items for the header region.
- $page['footer']: Items for the footer region.

Figure 4.10   Drupal variables for the page.tpl.php template

4.3.3.1   Adding variables to the basic page elements

As described on the Drupal documentation page, there are several variables available for building a page.tpl.php. The variables you chose to include depend on the functionality you desire for your theme. For example, if you chose to have breadcrumbs, add the $breadcrumbs variable, and if not leave them out.

Some of the most common variables in the page.tpl.php file are:

- $site_name
- $logo (the logo uploaded with theme settings; only useful when you're implementing the logo theme feature)
- $title (the page title)
- $main_menu
- $secondary_menu
- $breadcrumbs

There are also some variables associated with Drupal administration:

- $tabs (menu used for edit/view admin menus, among other things; often used by modules)
- $messages
- $action_links

Other useful variables include:
- $base_path (the path to your site root)
- $front_page (the path to the site front page)
- $directory (the path to your theme)

Variables are inserted using the *Render* API as follows:
```
<?php print render($tabs); ?>
```

If your PHP and HTML skills are above average you can obviously create a champion theme, by observing how the example was built and then using the permitted variables to build your own.

4.3.4   Building other template files

Similarly, there are default templates for other theme files which come with the Drupal core. A list of them can be found at the http://drupal.org/node/190815 (Core Templates).

With regards to the page.tpl.php file, the best way to build your own may be to find an existing core file, observe how it was put together and then build your own. For example, the node.tpl.php file for Garland looks like following:

```php
<?php
// $Id: node.tpl.php,v 1.24 2010/12/01 00:18:15 webchick Exp $
?>
<div id="node-<?php print $node->nid; ?>" class="<?php print
$classes; ?>"<?php print $attributes; ?>>

  <?php print $user_picture; ?>

  <?php print render($title_prefix); ?>
  <?php if (!$page): ?>
    <h2<?php print $title_attributes; ?>><a href="<?php print
$node_url; ?>"><?php print $title; ?></a></h2>
  <?php endif; ?>
  <?php print render($title_suffix); ?>

  <?php if ($display_submitted): ?>
    <span class="submitted"><?php print $submitted ?></span>
  <?php endif; ?>

  <div class="content clearfix"<?php print $content_attributes;
?>>
    <?php
    // We hide the comments and links now so that we can render
them later.
      hide($content['comments']);
      hide($content['links']);
      print render($content);
    ?>
  </div>

  <div class="clearfix">
    <?php if (!empty($content['links'])): ?>
      <div class="links"><?php print render($content['links']);
?></div>
    <?php endif; ?>

    <?php print render($content['comments']); ?>
```

```
      </div>

   </div>
```

Note this is just an HTML file with a PHP statements added in. The permitted values for the node.tpl.php file are provided in Figure 4.11.

node.tpl.php

Drupal 6   **Drupal 7**

View documentation   View source

Default theme implementation to display a node.

Available variables:

- $title: the (sanitized) title of the node.
- $content: An array of node items. Use render($content) to print them all, or print a subset such as render($content['field_example']). Use hide($content['field_example']) to temporarily suppress the printing of a given element.
- $user_picture: The node author's picture from user-picture.tpl.php.
- $date: Formatted creation date. Preprocess functions can reformat it by calling format_date() with the desired parameters on the $created variable.
- $name: Themed username of node author output from theme_username().
- $node_url: Direct url of the current node.
- $display_submitted: Whether submission information should be displayed.
- $submitted: Submission information created from $name and $date during template_preprocess_node().
- $classes: String of classes that can be used to style contextually through CSS. It can be manipulated through the variable $classes_array from preprocess functions. The default values can be one or more of the following:
    - node: The current template type, i.e., "theming hook".
    - node-[type]: The current node type. For example, if the node is a "Blog entry" it would result in "node-blog". Note that the machine name will often be in a short form of the human readable label.
    - node-teaser: Nodes in teaser form.
    - node-preview: Nodes in preview mode.
  The following are controlled through the node publishing options.
    - node-promoted: Nodes promoted to the front page.
    - node-sticky: Nodes ordered above other non-sticky nodes in teaser listings.
    - node-unpublished: Unpublished nodes visible only to administrators.
- $title_prefix (array): An array containing additional output populated by modules, intended to be displayed in front of the main title tag that appears in the template.
- $title_suffix (array): An array containing additional output populated by modules, intended to be displayed after the main title tag that appears in the template.

Other variables:

- $node: Full node object. Contains data that may not be safe.
- $type: Node type, i.e. story, page, blog, etc.
- $comment_count: Number of comments attached to the node.
- $uid: User ID of the node author.
- $created: Time the node was published formatted in Unix timestamp.
- $classes_array: Array of html class attribute values. It is flattened into a string within the variable $classes.
- $zebra: Outputs either "even" or "odd". Useful for zebra striping in teaser listings.
- $id: Position of the node. Increments each time it's output.

Node status variables:

- $view_mode: View mode, e.g. 'full', 'teaser'...
- $teaser: Flag for the teaser state (shortcut for $view_mode == 'teaser').
- $page: Flag for the full page state.
- $promote: Flag for front page promotion state.
- $sticky: Flags for sticky post setting.
- $status: Flag for published status.
- $comment: State of comment settings for the node.
- $readmore: Flags true if the teaser content of the node cannot hold the main body content.
- $is_front: Flags true when presented in the front page.
- $logged_in: Flags true when the current user is a logged-in member.
- $is_admin: Flags true when the current user is an administrator.

Field variables: for each field instance attached to the node a corresponding variable is defined, e.g. $node->body becomes $body. When needing to access a field's raw values, developers/themers are strongly encouraged to use these variables. Otherwise they will have to explicitly specify the desired field language, e.g. $node->body['en'], thus overriding any language negotiation rule that was previously applied.

Figure 4.11   Drupal variables for the node.tpl.php template

The allowable variables for use in theme files can be located at http://drupal.org/node/190815 (Core Templates).

4.3.5   Menus and theme settings

Even though blocks for the standard navigation menus, specifically the main menu and secondary menu are provided on the Blocks administration page, they are also considered variables. This means links for the main menu can be directly inserted in the page template, just by inserting the PHP variable for either of them wherever you want it displayed in the template.

This means you will not be able to move them around easily, except by working in the template. The same applies to other site elements such as the logo. The variable $logo can be directly placed in the theme. What this means is that the logo cannot be changed through the admin interface.

4.3.5.1   Print or render

Some variables need to be displayed using the render() function, while others can simply be printed. Knowing the difference is not difficult. If the variable is an array (as listed on the page.tpl.php reference page http://api.drupal.org/api/drupal/modules>system>page.tpl.php) you need to use render(). If not, the variable can be printed you (<?php print $variable; ?>).

If this persists to be a problem check the default page.tpl.php and see how they did it there.

4.3.6   Creating new theme regions

Any part of a page that you want to edit in the Blocks admin page, needs to be a region. Typically, this will include the header, right sidebar, content area, and footer. All the regions need to be introduced in the .info file, else they do not exist. If you don't declare any region in the .info file, Drupal will provide a set of default regions such as the header, highlighted, help, content, sidebar_first and sidebar_second.

Drupal 7 variables, including regions, are inserted using *render arrays*, which is a way of outputting regions and other elements into the page template. More information on this can be found at http://drupal.org/node/930760.

4.3.7   Content to regions

Regions are areas in a theme that are available for adding blocks and content to a web site. Drupal 7 adds *Highlighted* and *Help* as default regions. The Drupal 7 Bartik theme has following default regions:

```
regions[header] = Header
regions[help] = Help
regions[page_top] = Page top
regions[page_bottom] = Page bottom
regions[highlighted] = Highlighted

regions[featured] = Featured
regions[content] = Content
regions[sidebar_first] = Sidebar first
regions[sidebar_second] = Sidebar second

regions[triptych_first] = Triptych first
regions[triptych_middle] = Triptych middle
regions[triptych_last] = Triptych last

regions[footer_firstcolumn] = Footer first column
regions[footer_secondcolumn] = Footer second column
regions[footer_thirdcolumn] = Footer third column
regions[footer_fourthcolumn] = Footer fourth column
regions[footer] = Footer
```

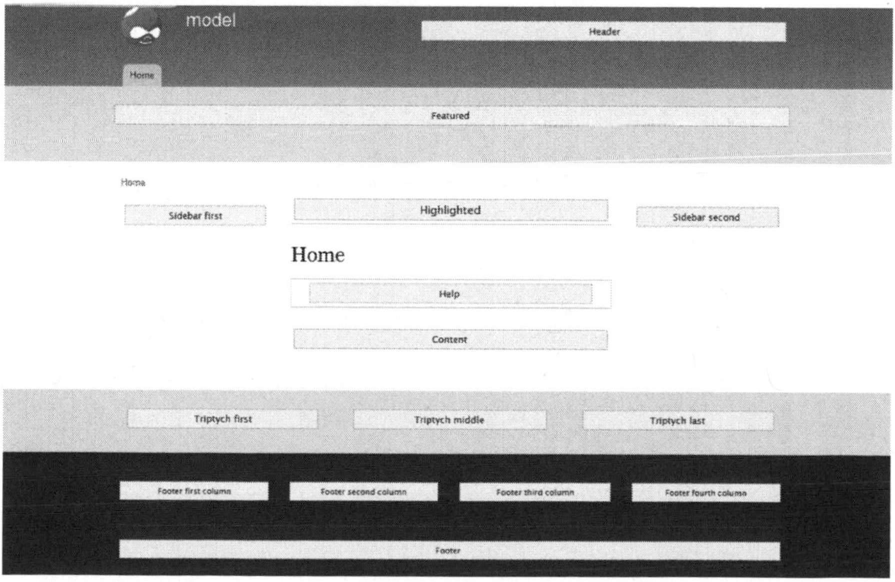

Figure 4.12   Available block regions for the Bartik theme

Figure 4.12 shows the position of the available block regions within the theme. Blocks of content can be manually placed in any of these positions through the blocks administration table. An example of this table for the Bartik theme is shown below Figure 4.13).

Figure 4.13   Blocks administration page for the Bartik theme

4.3.8   The header wrapper

For an example of how the code from the page.tpl.php file is graphically rendered, compare the image of the header portion of the Garland theme (Figure 4.14) to the code below.

Figure 4.14   Header portion of the Garland theme

```
<div id="header">
        <div id="logo-floater">
        <?php if ($logo || $site_title): ?>
          <?php if ($title): ?>
            <div id="branding"><strong><a href="<?php print
$front_page ?>">
                <?php if ($logo): ?>
                  <img src="<?php print $logo ?>" alt="<?php print
$site_name_and_slogan ?>" title="<?php print
$site_name_and_slogan ?>" id="logo" />
                <?php endif; ?>
                <?php print $site_html ?>
                </a></strong></div>
            <?php else: /* Use h1 when the content title is empty
*/ ?>
                <h1 id="branding"><a href="<?php print $front_page
?>">
                <?php if ($logo): ?>
                  <img src="<?php print $logo ?>" alt="<?php print
$site_name_and_slogan ?>" title="<?php print
$site_name_and_slogan ?>" id="logo" />
                <?php endif; ?>
                <?php print $site_html ?>
                </a></h1>
        <?php endif; ?>
        <?php endif; ?>
        </div>

        <?php if ($primary_nav): print $primary_nav; endif; ?>
```

```
        <?php if ($secondary_nav): print $secondary_nav; endif;
?>
        </div> <!-- /#header -->
```

It is quite easy to identify variables from the code for such elements as the logo [$logo], Site title [$site_title], Site name [$site_name_and_slogan], and several others.

4.3.9   The style.css file

In a static HTML page, a pointer needs to be placed within the page header to show the location of the stylesheet used for page display. An example pointer will look like the following:

```
<link rel="stylesheet" type="text/css" href="/model.css" />
```

This code tells the browser where the sylesheet (model.css) of the page that is being viewed is located. In a Drupal page, the source HTML will show similar references to stylesheets, but the difference is that those references are added automatically. The source will reveal that because of the granularity of the theme system, while some styles have been contributed by the theme, others have come from modules to provide the developer's styling for the module output.

As previously discussed, new styles can be added to a theme, and default styles can be overridden. In both cases the theme stylesheet must be entered in the .info file.

What goes into the stylesheet? The same sort of modular approach is used by the Drupal core for CSS classes as for standard page elements of the framework. Even though theme developers may create their own, a number of classes occur throughout a Drupal site. The following list may be used to understand where these classes occur and what they mean. A complete list of classes in Drupal 7 core can be found on the Drupal.org web site.

4.3.9.1   Page elements

Page elements should include the following:

- **.menu** All menu trees get this class, such as the navigation menu.
- **.block All blocks.** For more details about styling blocks see http://drupal.org/node/104319.

- **.links** Lists of links, including primary and secondary links in the page header, node links and taxonomy terms.
- **.element-hidden** The purpose of this class is to hide elements from users. Typically used to conceal elements which should not be immediately displayed to any user. An example would be a collapsible fieldset that will be expanded with a click from a user.
- **.element-invisible** The purpose of this of this class is to visually hide elements, but keep them available for screen-readers. Typically used for information required for screen-reader users. Not to be used for focusable elements, such as form elements and links because this causes issues for keyboard only or voice recognition users.
- **.element-invisible.element-focusable** The .element-focusable class extends the .element-invisible class to allow the element to be focusable when navigated to via the keyboard.

4.3.9.2   Node elements

- **.node** A wrapper DIV around all of a node, including its title.
- **.node-title** The title of the node.
- **.content** The body of the node. This will include additions other modules make, such as uploaded files or CCK fields.
- **.links** Applied to any URL that is a list of links, including primary and secondary links in the page header, and also node links and taxonomy terms. However, node links get the .links class on their enclosing DIV in the *style.css* file.
- **.terms** Taxonomy terms, which also get .links and .inline in the *style.css* file.
- **.inline** This is a system class for styling UI items into a horizontal line.
- **.feed-icon** RSS feed icons, are usually located at the foot of the page content area. To see how this is implemented in a stylesheet, look at the following example extracted from the stylesheeet for the Garland theme.

```
/**
 * Nodes & comments
 */
.node {
  border-bottom: 1px solid #e9eff3;
  margin: 0 -16px 1.5em;
```

```
      padding: 1.5em 16px;
  }

  ul.links li,
  ul.inline li {
    margin-left: 0;
    margin-right: 0;
    padding-left: 0; /* LTR */
    padding-right: 1em; /* LTR */
    background-image: none;
  }

  .node .links,
  .comment .links {
    text-align: left; /* LTR */
    padding-left: 0; /* LTR */
  }

  .user-picture,
  .comment .submitted {
    float: right; /* LTR */
    clear: right; /* LTR */
    padding-left: 1em; /* LTR */
  }

  .new {
    color: #ffae00;
    font-size: 0.92em;
    font-weight: bold;
    float: right; /* LTR */
  }

  .preview .node,
  .preview .comment,
  .node-sticky {
    margin: 0;
    padding: 0.5em 0;
    border: 0;
    background: 0;
  }

  .node-sticky {
```

```
    padding: 1em;
    background-color: #fff;
    border: 1px solid #e0e5fb;
    margin-bottom: 2em;
}

#comments {
    position: relative;
    top: -1px;
    border-bottom: 1px solid #e9eff3;
    margin: 1.5em -25px 0;
    padding: 0 25px;
}

#comments h2.comments {
    margin: 0 -25px;
    padding: .5em 25px;
    background: #fff url(images/gradient-inner.png) repeat-x 0 0;
}

.comment {
    margin: 0 -25px;
    padding: 1.5em 25px 1.5em;
    border-top: 1px solid #e9eff3;
}

.indented {
    margin-left: 25px; /* LTR */
}

.comment h3 a.active {
    color: #494949;
}

.node .content,
.comment .content {
    margin: 0.6em 0;
}
```

4.3.9.3   Theme tools

Several tools are available to assist you in customizing/building a theme for your site. They are contributed modules, the most popular of which are:

- Theme developer:
  http://drupal.org/project/devel_themer
- Theme generator:
  http://drupal.org/project/theme_generator
- Theme builder:
  http://drupal.org/project/themebuilder
- Theme editor:
  http://drupal.org/project/theme_editor

The theme builder module will only work with Drupal 6 although it can be used if you have little confidence with your PHP/HTML/CSS skills. If you chose this approach, it is possible to convert a Drupal 6 theme to Drupal 7. More details and step-by-step instructions can be found at http://drupal.org/update/themes/6/7.

4.3.10   Adding a screenshot

A screenshot roughly previews your finished theme and serves as an illustration to assist prospective users to decide if they want to use this theme. It will also be displayed on the *appearance* administration page. To create a screenshot, do a screen capture of your completed theme in a browser; then crop and resize it to a dimension of 294px x 219px, and save it as screenshot.png. Put this screenshot in the same folder as the .info file.

4.4   Summary

This chapter gives an overview of how the theme system functions. It explains the various components of a Drupal theme and how to determine which components are required or optional. The chapter shows how to proceed with the construction of a new theme from scratch, using the default PHPTemplate theme engine. This exercise looks at the typical structure of each of the component theme files and gives advice on how to create similar structures in a custom theme.

Chapter 5

Creating Drupal Modules

In Chapter 4 we discussed the essentials of building Drupal themes. The chapter looked briefly at the main components of a theme and how to create the look and feel of a Drupal site. We also learned how to build a theme from scratch using the PHPTemplate theme engine.

In this chapter we will similarly look at how to extend the functionality of a Drupal site through the development of a new module from scratch.

It is possible for a Drupal site to have three kinds of modules—core modules, contributed modules and custom modules. Core modules are those that come packaged with the basic Drupal install and have been approved by the Drupal team as well as the Drupal community. Contributed modules are those written by Drupal developers and shared for use with others under the GNU Public License (GPL). Custom modules on the other hand, are created by a developer for a specific site and may or may not be offered for public use. This chapter introduces you to creating custom Drupal modules.

This chapter is important for the following reasons:

- It enables the user to understand the structure of Drupal modules and their main building blocks.
- It enables the user build a module for a specific purpose on a Drupal site.

This chapter is a basic introduction to creating Drupal modules. It explains how to create an example module but does not address other matters such as theming the output of a module, nor does it address creating functionality in detail.

5.1   How modules function

A Drupal module is defined by a collection of PHP files which contain some level of functionality. Because the module code executes within the context of the site, it can use the functions, variables, and structures of the Drupal core. In fact, even though it may have an unusual file extension, the main module file is no different from any PHP file that can be independently created, tested and used to drive multiple functionality. This approach allows the Drupal core to call certain functions defined in specific places within modules to enhance the functionality of the core. The places where code can be executed are called *hooks* and are defined by a fixed interface (Figure 5.1).

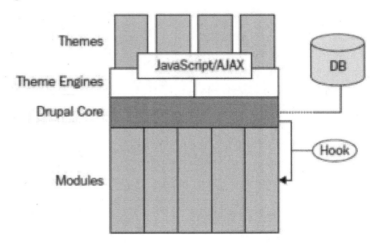

Figure 5.1   The Drupal schema

How does a module function within the larger Drupal framework? Modules are used to create functionality and they do this using *hooks*. For example, when Drupal receives a user request, it progressively loads critical libraries, themes, and modules and proceeds with mapping the URL requested to handle the code and format the output. These processes are done by means of hooks through which Drupal examines the currently installed and enabled modules to look for functions that follow a required pattern.

For example, when creating a page view, Drupal will look for modules which implement the *hook_block( )* and *hook_view ( )* functions and if these functions are found, it will execute them and then pass the data generated from the functions to create output for the user. Hooks will be discussed in a little more detail, shortly in section 5.1.6.

5.1.1   Components of a module

What would you find inside the folder of a typical module? The following example (Figure 5.2) from the *node* module file should give some indication:

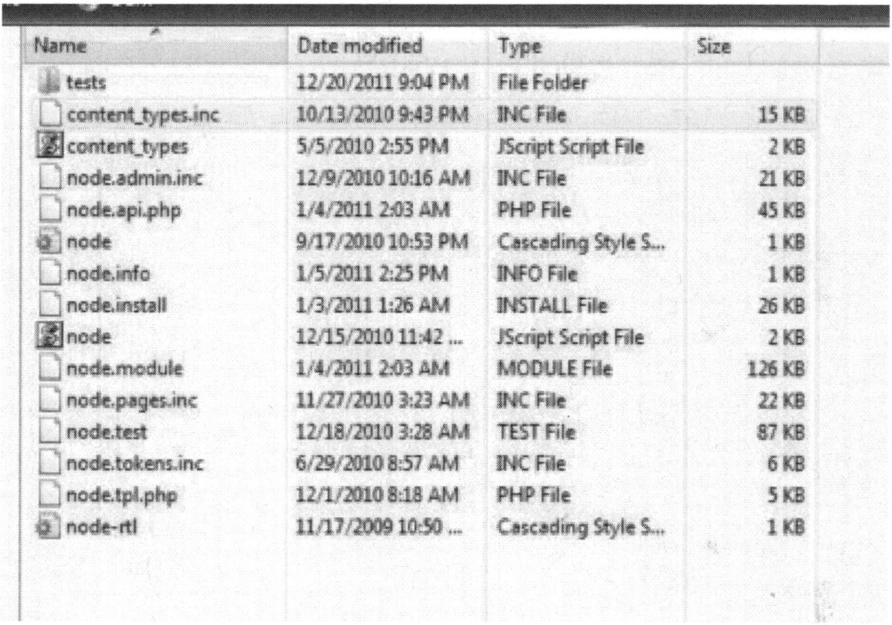

Figure 5.2   Example of module structure

Typically, a module needs to consist of two files, the *.info* file the *.module* file. The *.info* file is essential to define and declare the module and the *.module* file contains the functionality of the module. The example in Figure 5.2 contains helper files for the main .module file as well as styling files. None of these are absolutely required.

5.1.2   The .info file

It is required that all modules have a .info file extension. This file contains the metadata about the module. The general format and content of this file will look like the following (taken from the core node module).

```
; $Id: node.info,v 1.15 2010/12/20 19:59:42 webchick Exp $
name = Node
description = Allows content to be submitted to the site and
displayed on pages.
```

```
package = Core
version = VERSION
core = 7.x
files[] = node.module
files[] = node.test
required = TRUE
configure = admin/structure/types
stylesheets[all][] = node.css
```

Like the .info file for the themes, we will notice that the module .info file is merely a text file with a .info extension. Let's look at other possibilities for the content of the module *.info* file.

5.1.2.1   name (Required)

This is the name that will be displayed for your module. The naming convention should be in compliance with the Drupal capitalization standard. Only the first letter of the first word should be capitalized ("*Mynew module*", not "*mynew module*" or "*Mynew Module*").

Syntax:
```
name = Node
```

5.1.2.2   description (Required)

The description field should appear on the administration page, consist of not more than one line, and describe what the module does. This field is limited to 255 characters. Descriptions can contain links to documentation and sources. This is useful when online documentation is available and more informative than README files often supplied in a module folder.

Syntax (1):
```
description = Allows content to be submitted to the site and
displayed on pages.
```

Syntax (2):
```
description = Wildlife blog by <a href="http://
www.rotimiogunjobi.me.uk">Rotimi Ogunjobi</a>.
```

5.1.2.3   core (Required)

This entry is a declaration of the Drupal version your module is written for because a module created for one version of Drupal may not work with another version. If your module is written for Drupal 7, this value would be 7.x. Do not specify the minor version of a branch of Drupal in your description. You may state version 7.x but you may not specify version 7.3.

Syntax:
```
core = 7.x
```

5.1.2.4   files (Optional)

Any code files that contain class or interface declarations for modules, must be declared in the .info file. When a module is enabled, Drupal rescans all declared files, and indexes the interfaces and classes it finds.

Syntax:
```
files[] = node.test
```

5.1.2.5   dependencies (Optional)

There are options that appear in the .info file, one of which is module dependencies. If a module requires another module to be enabled, then each module must be listed. If dependencies are assigned for a module, Drupal will not allow it to be activated until the required dependencies are met.

Syntax:
```
dependencies[] = taxonomy
dependencies[] = CCK
```

5.1.2.6   package (Optional)

In the modules administration page, modules are listed according to categories. Thus, you will find that modules which are to be used together with any other installed modules would be listed together in the same category. If your module falls in the same category as others this should be declared in the .info file. If Drupal finds no association for your module in the .info file , it will simply be listed in the *Other* category.

Syntax.
```
package = "The desired grouping string"
```

5.1.3   The .module file

The .module file contains the functionality of the module either within the file itself or by calling functions and methods from other module files. Without the .module file, the module has no functionality at all and is not able to do anything at all other than be visible on the modules administration page.

5.1.4   General coding standards for modules

Before we start any serious coding, we must know that Drupal has thorough and strictly enforced coding standards to which all core code and add-on modules must adhere. Therefore, it may be a good idea to become familiarized with these coding standards which are documented at: http://drupal.org/coding-standards. Within this set of standards, several prominent ones should be brought to the fore.

5.1.4.1   Indenting and whitespace

You should always use an indent of 2 spaces, with no tabs; and all lines should have no trailing whitespace at the end.

5.1.4.2   Operators

All binary operators (operators such as +, −, =, !=, ==, >, etc.) should have a space before and after the operator for readability.

5.1.4.3   Casting

There should be a space between the (type) and the $variable in a cast:

```
(int) $mynumber.
```

5.1.4.4   Control structures

To distinguish control structures from function calls, control statements should have no more than one space between the opening parenthesis and the control keyword.

5.1.4.5   Line length and wrapping

Lines of code, except those ones containing function names, function/class definitions, variable declarations, etc, should not be longer than 80 chars.

5.1.4.6   Function calls

When functions are called, there should be no spaces between the function name, the opening parenthesis, and the first parameter. Spaces between commas and each parameter are permitted, with no space between the last parameter, the closing parenthesis, and the semicolon. Eg

```
$var = foo($bar, $baz, $quux);
```

5.1.4.7   Object instantiation

In order to maintain consistency between constructors that have arguments and default constructors, always include parentheses when instantiating objects.

```
$foo = new MyClassName();
$foo = new MyClassName($arg1, $arg2);
```

5.1.4.8   Arrays

Format arrays with a space separating each element (after the comma), and spaces around the => key assignment statement, if applicable:

```
$some_array = array('hello', 'world', 'foo' => 'bar');
```

5.1.4.9   Quotes

Drupal does not have a hard standard for the use of single quotes vs. double quotes. Where possible, maintain consistency within each module.

5.1.4.10   Including code

Anywhere you are unconditionally including a class file, use require_once(). Anywhere you are conditionally including a class file, use include_once(). Either of these will ensure that class files are included only once.

5.1.4.11   PHP code tags

Always use <?php ?> to delimit PHP code, not the shorthand, <? ?>. All module files which are PHP files and exclude the .info file and styling files, must start with an opening <? tag. However, Drupal coding standards http://drupal.org/node/318 require that the closing ?> tag be omitted. If this tag is included, runtime issues may result on some servers.

5.1.4.12   Semicolons

PHP requires semicolons at the end of most lines. However, you are permitted to omit them at the end of code blocks.

5.1.4.13   Functions and variables

The names of functions and variables should be in lowercase, and if the function name is a single word, the words should be separated with an underscore. Additionally, to avoid name collisions between modules, functions should have the grouping/module name as a prefix.

5.1.4.14   Constants

Constants should be all uppercase. If a constant is more than one word, these words should be separated with underscores.

5.1.4.15   Classes

Classes should be named using *CamelCase* standrds, For example:

```php
<?php
abstract class DatabaseConnection extends PDO {
?>
```

Class methods and properties should use "lowerCamelCase":

```php
<?php
public $lastStatement;
?>
```

5.1.4.16   File names

The names of document files should be all caps (e.g. README.txt) while the extension itself is lowercase (i.e. txt instead of TXT). All documentation files should have the file extension .txt.

5.1.5   Comments

There are two types of comments in Drupal code; in-line comments and headers. In-line comments are those that have been written within functions. Documentation on functions, constants, classes, etc., are extracted from the header comments using the Doxygen generation system. There is an excellent Doxygen manual on the Doxygen site http://www.stack.nl/~dimitri/doxygen/manual.html to help with this. The site provides information on the Drupal implementation of Doxygen, and the Drupal standards for both in-line and header comments.

5.1.6   How the hook functions

All functions that are directly used by Drupal modules are known as *hooks*. The syntax for including hooks in the module code is *{modulename}_{functionname}*. Here, "*functionname*" refers to a pre-defined function name suffix. An example of a complete hook is *{modulename}_hook_block_info*. Where the suffix "*hook_block_info*" refers to a Drupal module hook.

Figure 5.1 demonstrates that hooks are the means by which modules interact with the core code of Drupal. For example, hooks make the following possible:

- Enables a module to define new pages and URLs within the site by using the hook_menu.
- Makes it possible to add new content to pages by using the hook_block, hook_footer, etc.
- Makes it possible to set up custom database tables by using hook_schema.

The hooks provided in the Drupal core are listed at http://api.drupal.org/api/group/hooks. However, modules can define hooks of their own. For example, the hook_field_info hook is defined by the CCK module, but is a hook that can be used by modules that want to define a new type of content field. Typically, if a module defines a new hook, such modules would provide documentation about them.

Hooks can occur at various points in the thread of execution. In Drupal, an event should trigger an action. An event such as deleting a node should trigger the hook "hook_delete". Therefore, a hook can be thought of as an event listener. A partial list of core Drupal hooks is provided below (Figure 5.3). A complete list can be found at http://api.drupal.org/api/group/hooks.

5.2   Planning the module

Before you start to build a module, you should have a good idea of what it will do; you should also have good PHP coding skills. You will also have a development environment set up to see the progress and results of your work as you go along. An environment will be a working Drupal install, preferably on a local machine.

Functions & methods

Name	Description
hook_actions_delete	Executes code after an action is deleted.
hook_action_info	Declares information about actions.
hook_action_info_alter	Alters the actions declared by another module.
hook_admin_paths	Define administrative paths.
hook_admin_paths_alter	Redefine administrative paths defined by other modules.
hook_aggregator_fetch	Create an alternative fetcher for aggregator module.
hook_aggregator_fetch_info	Specify the title and short description of your fetcher.
hook_aggregator_parse	Create an alternative parser for aggregator module.
hook_aggregator_parse_info	Specify the title and short description of your parser.
hook_aggregator_process	Create a processor for aggregator module.
hook_aggregator_process_info	Specify the title and short description of your processor.
hook_aggregator_remove	Remove stored feed data.
hook_ajax_render_alter	Alter the commands that are sent to the user through the Ajax framework.
hook_archiver_info	Declare archivers to the system.
hook_archiver_info_alter	Alter archiver information declared by other modules.
hook_batch_alter	Alter batch information before a batch is processed.
hook_block_configure	Define a configuration form for a block.
hook_block_info	Define all blocks provided by the module.

Figure 5.3   Example Drupal hooks

In this chapter we will build a demonstration module which will do nothing spectacular other than show us how a module is constructed. We shall call this module "*demo*".

5.2.1   Naming the module

The first step in creating a module is to choose a *short name* for it. This short name will be used in all file and function names within the module. Coding standards require that it must start with a letter, and must contain only lower-case letters and underscores.

5.2.2   Create a folder

Where should we locate our module? The obvious answer is that it should go in the /modules folder with the core modules. However, we should never change the content of the /modules directory because any change will be overwritten when the Drupal installation I upgraded. Experienced users may advise that we place additional modules in the /sites/all/modules folder where Drupal places unmodified downloaded add-on modules. This makes sense because when the core is upgraded, this directory is not automatically overwritten. However, /sites/all/modules is not the recommended place to place custom modules in favor of the /sites/default/modules directory. This directory does not exist by default and must be created.

This method enables us to locate custom modules more easily. However, this may not be the most advantageous location in the case when our Drupal installation is configured to serve multiple sites. In which case, the /sites/default folder will be only available to the default site and none of the modules in that folder will be loaded for other sites. In our example, we will make use of the new sites/default/modules directory. Given our choice of short name is "*demo*", we will create a folder in our Drupal at: `sites/default /modules/demo`.

5.3   Creating the .info file

Once the *demo* folder has been created, we will create a new text file and save it as demo.info in the demo folder. Within the .info file in that folder, we will enter the following:

```
;$Id$
name = Demo
description = A simple demonstration module.
package = Demo
version = VERSION
core = 7.x
files[] = demo.module
```

This tells Drupal the name of the module, a description of what it does, and if the overall module package has any dependencies.

The first line is a standard inclusion, and it is the placeholder, where the version control system will store information about the file. Every module .info file should begin with Id. If you decide to contribute your module,

Drupal's CVS repository will automatically expand that line to something like:

```
;$Id: demo.info,v 1.1 2011/12/29 15:30:35 togunjobi Exp $
```

This indicates when the file was last checked into CVS, and who checked it in. Package will test the administrator and other modules the demo module is related to. For example, you will find core modules, grouped together under the Core package. Our demo module will be grouped under a new package called *Demo*.

What does Drupal do with the information you have supplied in the .info file? Figure 5.4 from the module administration page should give some indication.

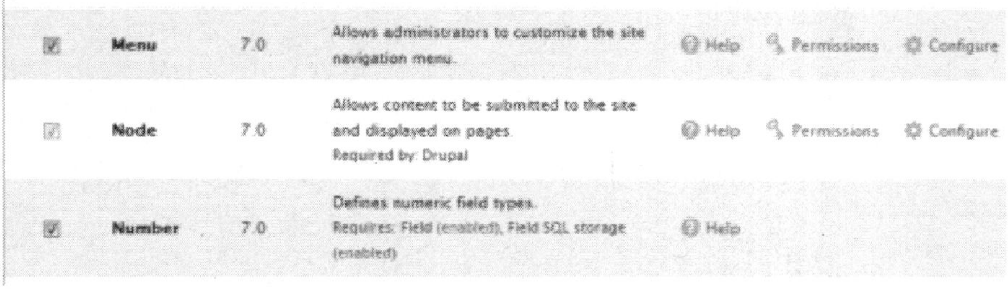

☑	**Menu**	7.0	Allows administrators to customize the site navigation menu.	⊘ Help	⚲ Permissions	⚙ Configure
☑	**Node**	7.0	Allows content to be submitted to the site and displayed on pages. Required by: Drupal	⊘ Help	⚲ Permissions	⚙ Configure
☑	**Number**	7.0	Defines numeric field types. Requires: Field (enabled), Field SQL storage (enabled)	⊘ Help		

Figure 5.4   Modules listed on the modules admin page

As for the .info file for the theme folder, note that everything from the line *"Information added by drupal.org packaging script on xxxx-xx-xx" and down is added by the drupal.org packaging script. The project and datestamp keys should never be manually added.*

5.4   Creating the .module file

In this section we will create a module file. With a text editor create a new file and save the file as demo.module. We will proceed to add basic function code to this file via the hook system.

5.4.1   Implementing the help hook

As we learned in earlier sections, hooks allow integration of a module with the actions of the Drupal core. The first hook we will implement while creating our module, will be *hook_help*, which is recommended for inclusion in all contributed Drupal modules. This hook provides help and additional information about the module to the administrator/user.

The method of implementing any hook in Drupal, is to replace "hook" in the hook name with your module's short name, and thereafter create a function in the .module file with that name. To implement hook_help() in the demo module, we first create a function called demo_help() in the demo.module file:

```php
<?php
function demo_help($path, $arg) {
}
?>
```

The $path parameter provides context for help and is recommended in order to process this variable with a switch statement. This code pattern is common in Drupal modules. The following is an abbreviated implementation of this help function for our demo.module, together with necessary comments:

```php
<?php
// $Id$
/**
 * @file
 * A simple demonstration module.
 *
 * This module provides a block that lists all of the
 * recent content.
 */
/**
 * Implements hook_help().
 */
function demo_help($path, $arg) {
  if ($path == 'admin/help#demo') {
    return t('A demonstration module.');
  }
}
```

The admin/help#modulename case is used by the Drupal core to link the main help page which is located at /admin/help or at ?q=admin/help. The help message provided above is A demonstration module, and you will eventually want to add more text to provide a better help content to the user. You should read the recommendations on the Drupal site at http://drupal.org/node/632280.

One of the strongest features of Drupal's internationalization and localization effort is that Drupal supports dozens of languages. .The *t()* function is responsible for translating strings from one language to another. It is required that you wrap every natural language string that may be displayed to a user, in the *t()* function.

When a t() function wraps text it marks it for translation and can give the code an added layer of security. Detailed information on this function may be found at the page http://api.drupal.org/api/function/t/7.

After we have created the help hook and saved the .module file, we now enable the module. A module needs two files to be recognized by Drupal: the .info and the .module file. Once we have created these files, we can enable the module (Figure 5.5).

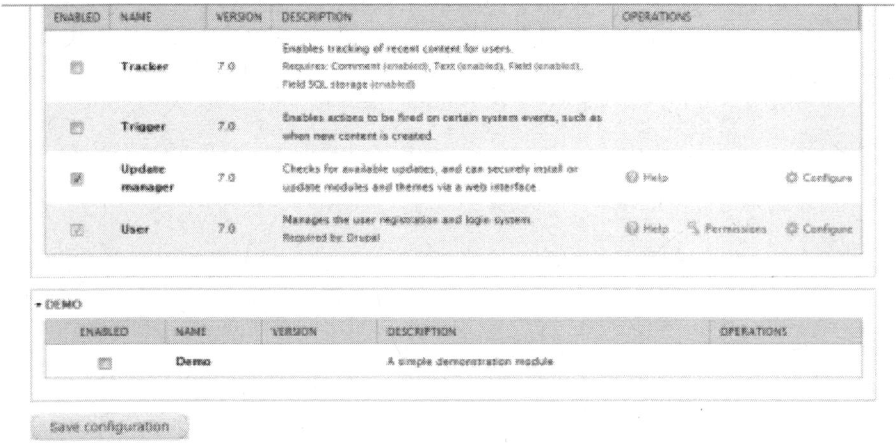

Figure 5.5   "DEMO" module shown on the modules page

Functions are added by adding the required hook and then with code (Figure 5.6). For example, if it is require to create a block view, we will be adding something similar to following.

```
/**
 * Implements hook_block_info().
 */
function demo_block_info() {
  $blocks[demo] = array(
  info' => t(Demo), //The name that will appear in the block
list.;
```

```
     'cache' => DRUPAL_CACHE_PER_ROLE, //Default
   );
   return $blocks;
}
```

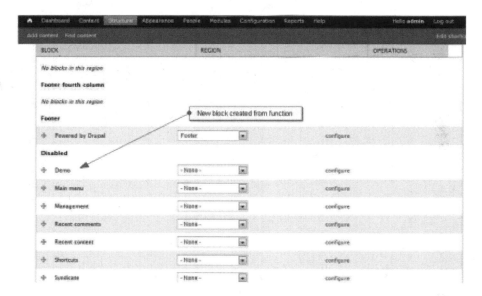

Figure 5.6   Block generated by "demo" module

5.5   Other module files

Notice there are other types of module files which need attention at this stage; specifically the .inc file and the .install file because they are not always required in a module.

5.5.1   .install files

A .install file is run the first time a module is enabled, and is used to run the setup procedures required by the module. The .install file does not have any special syntax. Installation instructions are enclosed in a hook_install() function. This hook is called when the module is first enabled. Any number of functions can reside here, but the most common task this file performs is creating database tables and fields. The .install files may also be used to perform updates whenever a new version of a module requires an update.

5.5.2   .inc file

Having a .inc file is a way to introduce greater flexibility in your coding and to make the performance of your module better, particularly if your module includes many functions. The .inc file permits hooks to be separated from functions. Thus, the function is not called by Drupal until a hook makes the demand for that event.

5.6   Testing and troubleshooting

Having concluded the coding for the demo module, we should test it.

5.6.1   Enable the module

On the modules administration page, you should see the new "demo" module in the demo category. Click the checkbox to enable *demo,* and save the configuration. Next to the module name there should be a *help option.* Clicking this option should provide the help text entered in demo_help.

5.6.2   Troubleshooting

As you add functions to your module file, along the way you may find things don't work as you expected as a result of syntax errors in the .module file. Syntax errors may occur from simple errors such as punctuation, semi-colons, commas, and incorrectly spelled hook names and module short names. Syntax errors will often cause a white screen to be displayed. When this occurs, the Apache error log will often reveal what the PHP error is. Also if you change the PHP error reporting level in the *Logging and Errors* administration page you your errors can be directly displayed *on screen* (Figure 5.7).

If you are unable to find and fix a syntax error in an enabled module, you may find that nothing on your site will be displayed. This is because Drupal will try to load your enabled module together with other enabled modules on every page request. The way to get your site working might be to completely delete the module's folder.

5.7   Resources for module development

Contributed modules exist which can make it easier to create a Drupal module. A few of them are provided here.

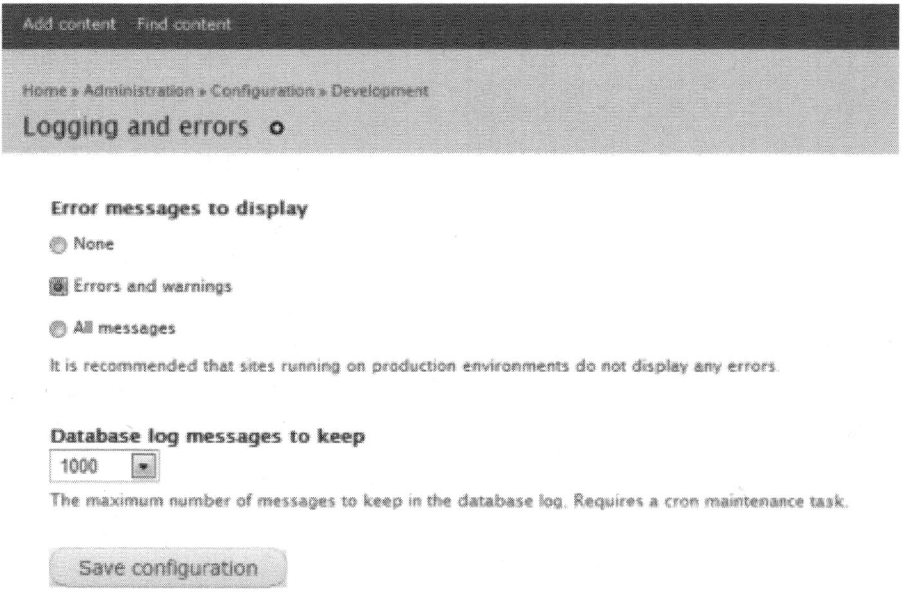

Figure 5.7   Logging and errors administration

- **Module Builder.** A module which auto-generates a skeleton or scaffolding for a module, along with hints on how to fill them in. http://drupal.org/project/module_builder
- **Coder.** Includes two developer modules that assist with code review and code manipulation. http://drupal.org/project/coder

5.8   Summary

In this chapter we learned the structure of a typical Drupal module and how to create a simple module which will list the current content of a Drupal site. We learned how to create:

- A .info file for describing the module
- A .module file for adding functionality to the module

We also learned how to test the resulting module and to troubleshoot if necessary. And we learned where to find a couple of resources which may help to rapidly develop a custom module.

Chapter 6

Building a Community Site with Drupal Commons

Community sites are places where people congregate to discuss and to share activities of mutual interests. In a typical community portal, people compose and share stories, including images, audio, and video, with other users. Not all community sites are public though; some exist as corporate intranets where access is not open over the internet. Intranet sites are especially useful for corporations that have personnel scattered over a wide geographical area. For such organizations, a well-designed community site could have the following visible benefits:

- Make their dispersed workforce more efficient.
- Help to socialize the corporate intranet to help employees identify experts, collaborate, and find information faster.
- Create a truly integrated workforce.

6.1 Acquia Drupal Commons

Commons is described as social business software that provides a content management system solution that is deeply integrated with the social web. Built on top of a Drupal framework, Commons comes ready to use out of the box with little configuration needed. With this software, anyone can quickly build and customize internal and external community websites. The Commons framework enables users to connect with friends, join groups, and create content. For developers, Commons enable you to build robust social applications and to create your own, branded social network. The Commons logo is shown in Figure 6.1.

6.1.1 Corporate community sites

Commons is especially useful for corporations that have personnel scattered over a wide geographical area that typically rely on email and phones to

Figure 6.1   Commons logo

communicate with one another. By creating a community site based on Commons social business software, all communications and information that need to be shared may be conveniently moved online.

Users may fill in their user profile with a photo and information about themselves so other community members can find them when they need their expertise. The ability to create Groups (which any site user may join) allows users to flock more closely together especially if they are working on the same or similar projects. Groups enable them to easily assemble themselves and the information that is useful to them.

Other useful tools are available to build and grow teams online. Users may create a blog post to say something on their own, start a forum discussion, create shared content using a wiki, let others know about upcoming activities by creating an event listing, set up a poll by asking questions, and use a micro blog for quick updates.

6.1.2   The benefits of Commons

Commons' collaborative environment enables productive interactions among employees, customers, and the web at a lower cost than most other solutions. Commons has the tools to make a dispersed workforce more efficient. It may be used to socialize the corporate intranet to help employees identify experts, collaborate, find information faster, and thus create a truly integrated workforce. Since Commons is based on the Drupal platform, if you need functionality that isn't natively provided, additional modules can be implemented from the Drupal community.

6.1.3   Drupal Commons support

Commons was created and is supported by Acquia—a company that provides enterprise grade support and cloud hosting that complement Commons perfectly. Although an ordinary Commons site is free to use,

Acquia can provide custom site development, hosting, and maintenance services.

6.2   Installation

Installation of Drupal Commons is an easy process, but could take a bit of time because of the large number of modules that need to be installed, enabled, and configured. The installation environment is also very important, otherwise the installation will fail. Please keep the following in mind regarding the installation environment:

- Ensure that PHP is configured with the following settings:
  - max_execution_time is greater than or equal to 120 seconds
  - memory_limit is greater than or equal to 128 MB (190 MB recommended)
  - mod_rewrite is enabled
- Ensure that the GD graphics library is installed for PHP.

The installation file can be downloaded at the Acquia web site (https://www.acquia.com/downloads).

After the download, the content of the Commons distribution file should be extracted to your web server. Similar to installing an ordinary Drupal site, make a copy of the file sites/default/default.settings.php and rename it sites/default/settings.php. Thereafter ensure that the permissions of the file /sites/default.settings.php provide the web server write privileges to the file.

Since Acquia Commons is built on Drupal 6, the installation is similar to installing Drupal 6, and which you will find in Chapter 1 of this book. The starting page in the installation process is shown in Figure 6.2. From this screen, select the Commons installation profile and click Save and continue.

6.3   Features

During the installation process you will be presented with a screen asking what features you will wish installed. Commons comes programmed with many features that are really just pre-packaged modules, or functionality made possible by combinations of those modules (Figure 6.3).

It is suggested to install the following features at a minimum:

Figure 6.2   Installation start page

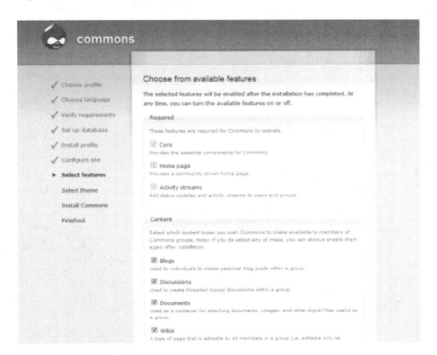

Figure 6.3   Select initial features to install

- **Core.** In Acquia Commons, the required features and modules include the core Drupal files as well as Home page and Activity streams. These cannot be disabled from the installation screen.
- **Home page.** The Home page is a feature that provides a community driven home page. If this feature is disabled, the Home page is not available for the site users, and is not visible on the main navigation menu.
- **Activity streams.** This feature enables users to communicate with others both publicly and privately without having to create formal content. This is an alternative communication method for users to create status messages in their activity stream, their friends' activity streams or group activity streams. If this feature is disabled the accompanying functionality is also disabled.

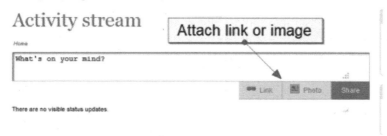

Figure 6.4   Activity stream create

6.4   Optional features

Apart from the required features and modules, the following optional content types are available from the installation profile.

- **Blogs.** A blog is a personalized post made by a user and this feature enables users to create single-post blog entries into groups.
- **Discussions.** Discussions are threaded posts made into a forum. If this feature is installed, users will be able to create discussions in groups (Figure 6.5).
- **Documents.** Uploading files to a Drupal site is not enabled by default. If this feature is enabled, users will be able to upload document, image, compressed and other permitted file types into groups. If disabled, users will only be able to upload supported image files to groups.

Figure 6.5   Discussions page

- **Wikis.** Wikis are a topical content type with shared ownership which users are jointly permitted to create and edit. This feature will enable your users to create wiki pages in groups.
- **Polls.** A poll is typically be used to collect the views of other users concerning a particular issue, usually with multiple-choice questions. Users will be able to create polls in groups if this feature is enabled.
- **Events and calendars.** An event is an activity with a defined period of time, which is represented in a calendar. If this feature is enabled, users will be able to create event calendars in groups (Figure 6.6).

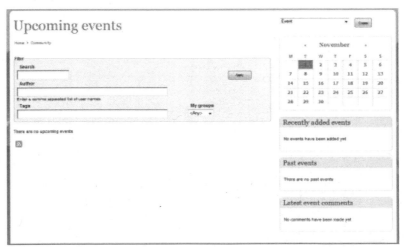

Figure 6.6   Upcoming events page

- **Social profiles.** This feature enables the display of more detailed Commons social profile information for users. If disabled, only the default profile information will be shown and items such as following will not be available:
    - Recent activity
    - About
    - My groups block
    - Edit my profile link

Figure 6.7   User profile page

- **Subgroups.** Groups are probably one of the most important features of Commons. The feature permits users to create groups based on specific interest. When this feature is enabled, groups can be organized into a hierarchy of groups within other groups. If disabled it is not possible to configure a group to contain another group, and the existing group hierarchy will be displayed as a single level.
- **Notification.** Users may wish to receive updates on content posted to a content area, on a subject, or by another user. When this feature is enabled, users will be sent email notifications for site activity in areas that they have specifically requested updates.
- **User awards.** A good way to grow a community site is to reward users for their activity via a reputation system that awards points and badges for community involvement. Enabling this feature displays points or badges that users have earned for their participation on the site.

- **Community invitation.** Another good way to grow a community site is to allow users to invite other users to join the website. When enabled, this feature provides a Invite a friend link on the users' profile pages.
- **Content aggregator.** This feature adds RSS feeds to groups, and the group navigation bars displays a Feeds tab.
- **SEO.** This feature combines all SEO-oriented capabilities and makes them available for use.
- **Acquia Network subscription.** The Acquia Network feature provides additional services to a Commons site, including enhanced site search and spam protection. If this feature is enabled users receive a free 30-day trial of Acquia Network. Optionally, users can enter a key for an existing Acquia Network subscription.

6.5   Themes

After selecting the features and profile to be installed, you will be presented with another screen that shows a set of themes available in your Commons package. The theme you select will apply to the look of your site when installed. The selection you make at this stage can be changed later (Figure 6.8).

Figure 6.8   Theme administration page

6.6   The installed site

After the Commons site installation has been installed, you will be given an option to visit your user page and alternatively presented with a link leading to the front page. Depending on the features and the theme selected, the site should look something like Figure 6.9. Congratulations, your community site is nearly ready for use.

Figure 6.9   Activity stream on front page

6.7   Configuration

After concluding the installation of a new community site, some additional configuration is necessary to customize it to suit your needs. Examples include changing the header graphic, creating or changing groups, events, the overall visual appearance of the site, the layout of individual website pages, etc. Although Acquia offers dedicated training programs for this, a few customizations are provided in the following sections.

6.7.1   Changing the header graphic

By default, a new Commons site has a Commons logo at the top. You may wish to replace it with your company or organizations' logo. To do this, you need to be logged into the site with administrative privileges. Click the tool icon in the upper-left corner of the web page (Figure 6.10) to open the administrative menu.

Figure 6.10   Administrative tools Icon

1.   From the administrative menu, select **Administer>Site building>Themes** to open the Themes page.

2.   Locate the theme with the *Default* option selected, and then click the **configure** link for that theme.

3.   Scroll down to the Logo image settings section, and browse to your logo in the **Upload logo image** field.

4.   After you upload your logo, click **Save configuration**.

The website home page and all of its subpages now display the new logo (Figure 6.11).

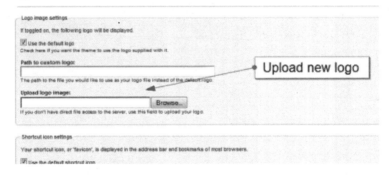

Figure 6.11   Changing the site logo

6.7.2   Changing the home page introductory block

The default home page has a block at the top that says "Community Powered Innovation." It includes information about Commons for the site administrator. One of the first things you'll want to do is to modify the default content on the home page to reflect your own organization, or the purpose of your site. To modify the text in the block that currently says "Community Powered Innovation," complete the following steps:

1. Hover the cursor over the "Community Powered Innovation" block. You'll notice that a gear icon appears in the upper-right corner of the block (Figure 6.12).

Figure 6.12   Contextual link icon for editing block content

2. Click the gear. The *'Homepage Commons information'* block page opens (Figure 6.13).

3. Scroll down the page to the **Box body** field, and then replace the content with the welcome message for your new website. You can format the content in this field using the formatting toolbar at the top of the field.

4. After you change the content, click **Save Block**.

5. Your new welcome message is now on the home page for your visitors to see.

'Homepage Commons information' block

Home > Administer > Site building > Blocks

Block specific settings

Box description: *
Homepage Commons information
A brief description of your box.

Box title:
Community Powered Innovation
The title of the box as shown to the user.

Box body:
```
<h3>Customize your site</h3>
Add your own look &amp; feel, configure how it works, or
extend it by installing more Drupal modules.
</div>

<div class="intro-textblock">
<h3>Link in the Network</h3>
```
The content of the block as shown to the user.

Change block HTML

Input format

○ Filtered HTML

Figure 6.13   Editing block details

6.7.3   Adding a page to the website outside of a group

If you have a specific web page that you do not want to include in a group, such as an "About Us" page, administrative users can create a normal web page, and then add it to the navigation menu. To create a web page, complete the following steps:

1. Click the tool icon in the upper-left corner of the web page.

2. The administrative menu appears as a black bar on the left of the page.

3. From the admin menu, select **Create content>Page**. The *Create Page* opens.

4. In the **Title** field, enter the title of the page. This title appears in the page header and in the browser title bar.

5. Create content for the page in the **Body** field. You can format the content in this field using the formatting toolbar at the top of the field.

6. In the **Menu link title** field, enter the name that you want to appear in the menu.

7. Examine the **Parent item** field. The default value is *Primary links*, which means that this menu item will appear on the top navigation menu.

8. Click **Save**.

6.7.4   Changing order in the navigation menu

Commons displays your new menu entry in the main navigation menu. Notice that it is at the right-most position. To change the order of items in a navigation menu, complete the following steps:

1. From the administrative menu, select **Administer>Site building>Menus**. The Menus page opens.

2. Click the **Primary links** link. The Primary links page opens.

3. Your new menu item is at the top of the list of menu items for the main navigation menu. To move your menu entry to another location, grab the arrow icon to the left of the menu entry and drag it to the new location in the menu.

4.   Note that you can either make your menu entry a top-level entry for this menu, or you can make it an entry in a drop-down entry for one of the other menu entries.

5.   After you move your menu entry to the correct location, click *Save configuration.*

6.   Your new page is now available to all of your visitors as a menu option on the main navigation menu in the position that you set.

6.8   Administration

Basic administration in a Commons site is really no different from a regular Drupal 6 site However, in Commons there are a whole lot of extra features that need to be administered and these include subgroups, activity streams, status messages and sending messages to other users.

6.8.1   Subgroups

A community of users is usually more than what a single level of groups can fully provide for. To provide more flexibility, Commons now supports subgroups, or groups within groups.

6.8.1.1   Configuring subgroups

To configure how Commons handles the subgroups on your site, complete the following steps:

1.   To open the administrative menu, click the tool icon in the upper left corner of the page.

2.   From the administrative menu, select *Administer>Organic groups>Subgroups configuration* (**Figure 6.14**). The Subgroups configuration page opens. This page allows you to set the site-wide preferences for how Commons handles the following functions in the group hierarchy:

   - **Content propagation**. How content is propagated amount groups. If all checkboxes are unchecked, content is not propagated.

   - **Subscribing members**. How user memberships are propagated among groups. If all checkboxes are unchecked, memberships are not propagated.

- **Unsubscribing members**. How user membership removals are propagated among groups. If all checkboxes are unchecked, propagation does not happen when unsubscribing memberships.

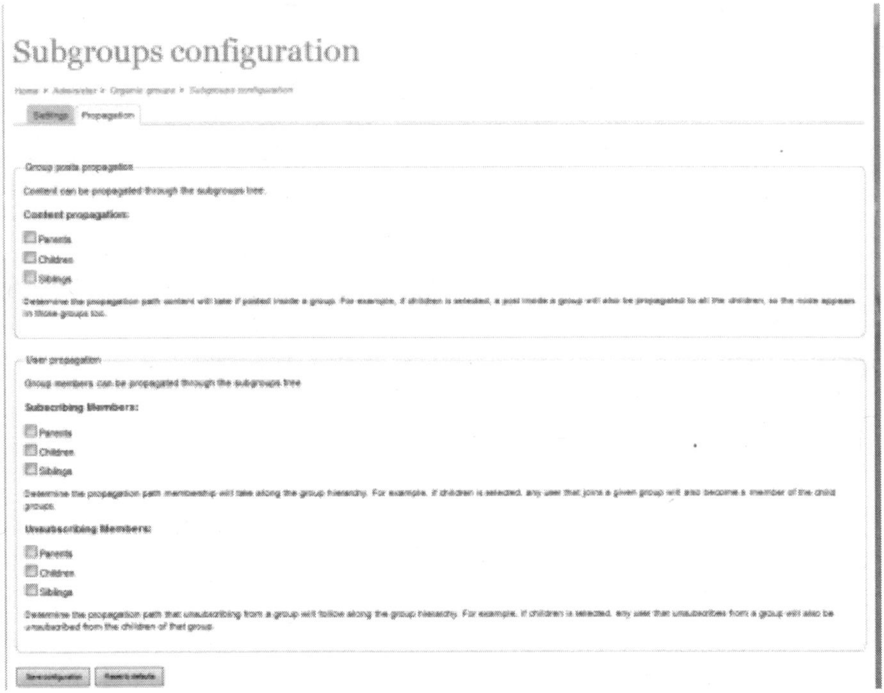

Figure 6.14   Subgroup configuration page

6.8.1.2   Creating a subgroup

Create a group. To do this,

1.   Select **Community>Groups** from the primary links menu and then click **Create a group.**

2.   Before you save the group, scroll down to the **Parent** vertical tab, and select the parent group for this subgroup from the **Parent** drop-down menu.

3.   Click **Save**.

6.8.1.3   Merging two subgroups

View a list of your groups. To do this,

1. Select *My stuff>My groups* from the primary links menu.

2. Ensure that the groups you want to merge have the same parent group, and then click the link for one of the groups that you want to merge.

3. Click the *Edit* tab.

4. Scroll to the bottom of the page, and then click *Delete*.

5. On the confirmation page, select the "Do nothing" option to keep your group posts, and then click *Delete Group*.

6.8.1.4   Deleting a subgroup

View a list of your groups. To do this,

1. select *My stuff>My groups* from the primary links menu.

2. Click the link for the group that you want to delete, and then click the Edit tab.

3. Scroll to the bottom of the page, and then click *Delete*.

4. On the confirmation page, determine if you want to keep all posts in the group (they'll be moved to another community in the group hierarchy) or to delete posts that only belong to this group.

5. Click *Delete Group*.

Note: If you delete the parent group of a subgroup, any children subgroups inherit the deleted group's parent group as their new parent, and move up the hierarchy to replace the deleted group.

6.8.2   Activity streams

Commons now provides you and your users more avenues of communication by using activity streams. By creating status messages in their own or their friends' profiles' activity streams, users can communicate with others both publicly and privately without having to explicitly create formal content. Along with user-created status messages, Commons can display a user's activity, including content creation and group membership changes.

6.8.2.1   Configuring activity streams

You can configure Commons to track several different kinds of user and group activity to display on the status wall.

1.   To open the administrative menu, click the tool icon in the upper left corner of the page.

2.   From the admin menu, select **Administer>Rules>Triggered rules**. The Triggered rules page opens.

3.   Use this page to manage the activity streams that Commons tracks and displays.

6.8.2.2   Viewing activity streams

To view a user's activity, including blog entries, editing a wiki, or joining a group, open their user profile and inspect their status wall. You can see a group's activity stream by opening the group, and viewing the list of recent activities relating to the group.

6.8.3   Creating a status message

To create a new status message do the following :

1.   Open your profile page. Note that your profile page has a blank text field with a **Share** button (Figure 6.15).

Figure 6.15   Creating status message

2.   Enter a status message. Your friends will see this message on their status wall and on your profile page.

3.   If you want to share a web link, click the link icon (Figure 6.16).

4.   Enter the URL that you want to share. If more than one image appears for the link, click on the left/right arrows to select

Figure 6.16   Selecting status message link image

> another image. If you don't want to display an image for the link, check the No thumbnail checkbox.

5.   To share the link, click Attach.

6.   If you want to share an image, click the image icon. To find an image on your computer, click Browse.

7.   Click Share. The new status message appears on your profile page.

6.8.4   Sending messages to other users

To send a message to another user do the following:

1.   Open the target user's profile page. To do this, select ***Community>Members*** from the primary links menu, browse to the user, and then click on their profile. Note that the profile page has a blank text field with a ***Share*** button (Figure 6.17).

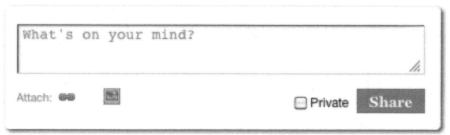

Figure 6.17   Sharing messages with other users

2.   In the status field, enter a message you want to send to the user.

3. To make this message only visible to you and the user, check the *Private* checkbox.

4. Click *Share*.

The new status message appears on the user's profile page.

6.8.5   Posting messages to a group

To post a message to a group do the following :

1. Open the group page. To do this, select *My stuff>My groups* from the primary links menu, and then click the link for a group. Note that the group page has a blank text field with a *Share* button.

2. Enter a status message.

3. Click *Share*.

The new status message appears on the group page, as well as the profile page of any user that is a member of this group.

6.9   Building Administrative Skills

A Drupal Commons site can be customized in many other ways, including changing the overall visual appearance via creating new themes, and changing the layout of individual website pages. Additional training to help you accomplish these more advanced actions is available from Acquia, who offer on-site classroom style courses that can meet these needs. More information can be obtained from the Acquia web site (http://www.acquia.com).

6.10   Summary

This chapter shows how to install and to do basic configuration of a community site built with the Acquia Commons development framework. It shows the different stages of the installation process and identifies the various features that are available. It concludes with showing where users can get more advice and assistance on how to perform advanced administrative operations on the Commons site.

Chapter 7

Building a Conference Site with COD

Corporate bodies, societies, clubs often need to organize conferences and seminars especially for members and staff. The traditional way has been to mail out conference brochures and registration forms and to conclude fulfillment by phone or mail. Nowadays, conferences are getting more technical. For societies with thousands of members scattered all over the world, members are seeking to be involved in the selection of the content of their training conferences. Therefore, having a web interface which serves as a hub for the organization, arrangement, and registration for conferences is now making good sense. A well-designed conference site may add the following benefits to the implementation of a conference:

- Permit participants to have a say on resources
- Permit online registration and fulfillment
- Socialize the participants by permitting them to be pre-acquainted before the conference begins
- Save cost on correspondence between organizers and participants

7.1 Acquia COD

COD is an acronym for Conference Organizing Distribution. This is a Drupal distribution developed specially and primarily for building and running a conference, BarCamp, or event website. The website http://www.useCOD.com shows an outline of features provided by this software. These include tools and interfaces for organizing conference resources and for displaying them. The shopping cart feature also makes it possible for attendees to select what resources and other conference related products they wish to purchase and pay for them online.

COD is an open source project which was initially created by a Growing Venture Solutions (GVS) and has now been taken over by Acquia. Offered free to download and to use, COD is used by a long list of sites including several Drupal Camps and DrupalCons. COD was created on a Drupal framework and at the time of this writing is only available with Drupal 6.

COD is supported by Acquia—a company that provides enterprise grade support and cloud hosting for COD sites. And although it is free to use, Acquia can provide custom COD development. Refer to Figure 7.1 for the COD logo.

Figure 7.1   COD Logo

7.1.1 COD Benefits

Several out-of-the box features are offered by the COD distribution of Drupal. These include conference registration features, conference session tools, and sponsor management features. These features make COD a versatile application for anyone desiring to build and run a conference or events site. The following advantages can be obtained from COD out-of-the -box:

- A complete conference and event site that can be customized and themed to meet user requirements
- The ability to sell event tickets and perform attendee registration activities. COD has includes e-commerce capabilities and permits selling workshop attendance as well as physical goods.
- User-submitted sessions/talks can be collected online, and made available for attendees to vote on. This helps organizers assess the popularity of each proposed session.
- A robust and configurable event schedule, displaying multiple tracks
- Sponsors' logos and names can be collected online, displayed in block positions, and linked to sponsor pages.

7.2 Installing COD

The installation environment for COD should have the following as a minimum configuration:

- PHP 5.2
- MySQL 5
- Apache
- Apache mod_rewrite module enabled for clean urls

In general, COD should work with the same general system requirements that you will use for Drupal 6.

7.2.1   Obtaining COD

As suggested by the project maintainers, there are three main ways to obtain COD:

- **The speedy method.** Download the packaged COD distribution from the project site.
- **The command line method.** Build it yourself using Drush and Drush Make.
- **The module-by-module method.** Download the individual cod_support modules.

7.2.1.1   Downloading the COD distribution

This is the method recommended by the project owners. What can be appreciated from the onset is that the distribution is as easy to install as core Drupal. It is packaged with Drupal core, as well as all required modules and libraries that make up the COD profile. Therefore, if you can install Drupal, you can install COD.

However, the drawback of using this method is that when improvements are made to the distribution package, and this occurs every few months, you may not get the benefit of improvements made since the latest package was created. The installation file can be downloaded at the useCOD web site: http://usecod.com/cod/cod-7.x-1.0-beta2.tar.gz

7.2.1.2   Building by using Drush and Drush Make

This is a more difficult method and requires that you have sufficient knowledge of how to use the following:

- The *nix command-line interface
- Drush
- Drush Make

This method downloads COD and all dependencies through Drush. The advantage here is that it enables you preview upcoming features in a development version of COD. If you aim to use this method, you will find the following links very useful:

- Drush : http://drupal.org/project/drush
- Drush Make: http://drupal.org/project/drush_make
- Cod stable make file: http://drupalcode.org/project/cod.git/history/refs/heads/6.x-1.x:/cod.make
- Cod make file for developers: http://drupalcode.org/project/cod.git/history/refs/heads/6.x-1.x:/cod-dev.make

7.2.1.3   Downloading the individual cod_support modules

This method provides the greatest level of installation flexibility. The COD functionality is implemented by the cod_support modules which can be separately downloaded from the cod_support project (http://drupal.org/project/cod_support).

Cloning COD from Git (http://drupal.org/project/cod_support/git-instructions) or using the development snapshot, will provide the latest version of these features. After downloading the cod_support modules, the features you want can be enabled by using the Features module interface at admin/build/features. The Features module enables the capture and management of Drupal features. A feature is defined as a collection of Drupal entities which together satisfy a certain use-case. Examples of features could be a blog, image gallery or e-commerce store.

The advantage of using this method is that COD can be built over an existing Drupal site. The disadvantage is that many module dependencies will also need to be downloaded and installed in order for COD to work.

7.2.1.4   Completing the installation

COD can be installed as you would install any other Drupal 6 site. However, you need though to choose "Conference Organizing Distribution" as the installation profile.

After the installation has completed, the default home page will be the COD configuration instructions node. You will need to demote the default home page from the front page before making the site available to users. It should be replaced with a new home page created by promoting another node to the front page or by using Views or Panels or both (Figure 7.2).

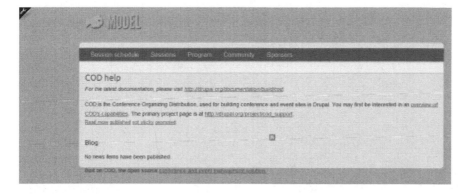

Figure 7.2 COD default front page

7.3 Preliminary configuration

After concluding the installation of your new community site you need to do some configuration, to make it look more like what you want. This involves changing the header graphic, creating new roles, changing the site theme, and so on.

To do this, you need to be logged into the web site with administrative privileges. After this, click the tool icon in the upper-left corner of the web page (Figure 7.3).

Figure 7.3 Administrative tools icon

This will open up the Administrator's Panel as a black panel on the left of the page (Figure 7.4). The Administrator's Panel has several tabs each containing a group of links. The main tabs are:

- **My Account.** Contains links to the administrative user account
- **Administer.** Contains links, to the administration sections of your Drupal framework.
- **Conference management.** Contains links to managing functions such as speakers, sessions, sponsors and other conference resources.
- **Create content.** Contains links to create new site content

- Conference management - containing links, to managing functions such as speakers, sessions, sponsors and other conference resources.
- My account – containing links to the admin user's account

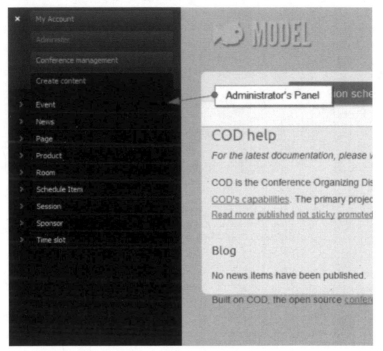

Figure 7.4   Administrator's side panel

7.3.1   Changing the header graphic

By default, the newly installed COD site has a fish symbol logo at the top. You may wish to replace this with the logo of your conference or organization.

To do this, select *Administer>Site building>Themes*, from the Administrator's Panel. This will open the themes administration page.

- Locate the theme with the "Default" option selected, and click the configure link for that theme.
- Scroll down the page to the Logo image settings section, and upload your logo in the Upload logo image field.
- After you have uploaded your logo, click Save configuration.

Your website home page and all of its subpages now display the new logo.

7.3.2   Changing themes

To change the theme, you also need to do this from the *Administer>Site building>Themes page*. For instructions on how to upload fresh themes, refer to preceding chapter on administering a Drupal site. The theme you select affects the look of the site and can be changed at any time.

7.3.3   Creating roles and permissions

Some user roles are automatically created during installation. These include the site administrator, attendee manager, session organizer and sponsor organizer roles. It may be necessary to add additional roles, such as attendee and speaker, depending on how people are expected to interact with the site. You can edit roles anytime. To do this, go to the *AdministerUser Management> Roles* page.

COD is restrictive with permissions and therefore you will need to adjust permissions as needed. For example, the posting of comments are disabled by default on content types such as events, sponsors, rooms, time slots, and schedule items. You may change these as you wish.

7.3.4   Cart Settings

The Ubercart shopping cart which ships with COD is an extremely powerful and versatile e-commerce module and probably the best available for use with Drupal. However, Ubercart requires configuration, much of which is accomplished with the installation scripts in COD. To get the most out of Ubercart, you need to do some additional customization to make it belong wholly to your site.

Store settings and payment settings are especially important. These can be accessed through the Configuration page located at *Admin>Store administration>Configuration* or at http://yoursite/?q=admin/store/settings (Figure 7.5).

7.3.4.1   Store settings
The store settings pages are the places where you enter information such as store contact details, store displays, currency, weight and dimension

Configuration

Cart settings
Configure the cart settings.
Checkout settings
Configure the checkout settings.
Country settings
Configure country specific settings.
Order settings
Configure the order settings.
Payment settings
Configure the payment settings.
Price handler settings
Select which price handlers to use for your store.
Product settings
Configure product settings.
Store settings
Configure the main store settings.

Store settings

Figure 7.5   Store configuration page

formats. You can access these setting via the store configuration page or at *Admin>Store administration>Configuration>Store settings* (Figure 7.6).

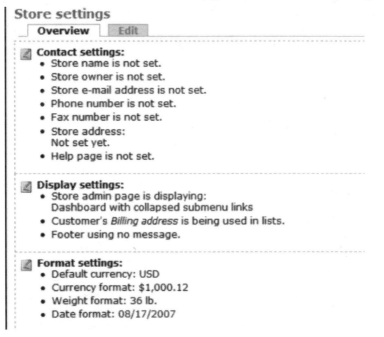

Store settings

| **Overview** | Edit |

Contact settings:
- Store name is not set.
- Store owner is not set.
- Store e-mail address is not set.
- Phone number is not set.
- Fax number is not set.
- Store address:
  Not set yet.
- Help page is not set.

Display settings:
- Store admin page is displaying:
  Dashboard with collapsed submenu links
- Customer's *Billing address* is being used in lists.
- Footer using no message.

Format settings:
- Default currency: USD
- Currency format: $1,000.12
- Weight format: 36 lb.
- Date format: 08/17/2007

Figure 7.6   Store settings panel

7.3.4.2   Payment settings

Payment settings concern matters such as how events and conference associated products are to be paid for. Payment methods are not provided by default when COD is installed. To select the payment gateway options for your site, go to the modules admin page, and select the desired payment methods (Figure 7.7). The available payment options are Paypal, credit card, Cybersource, Googlecheckout, 2Checkout, and Authoize.net. The Ubercart project site has contributed modules that provide other payment gateways (http://www.ubercart.org/contrib).

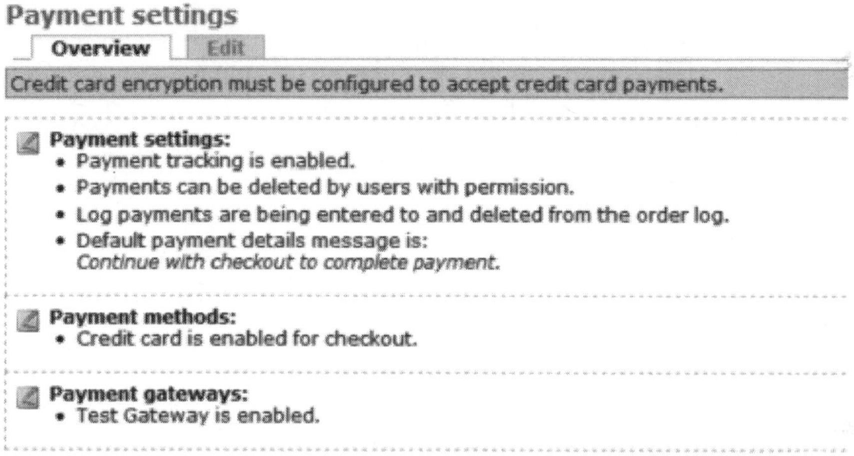

Payment settings

Overview | Edit

Credit card encryption must be configured to accept credit card payments.

Payment settings:
* Payment tracking is enabled.
* Payments can be deleted by users with permission.
* Log payments are being entered to and deleted from the order log.
* Default payment details message is:
  Continue with checkout to complete payment.

Payment methods:
* Credit card is enabled for checkout.

Payment gateways:
* Test Gateway is enabled.

Figure 7.7   Payment settings panel

7.4   Features

If you are familiar enough with Drupal framework, you will not find it difficult to see that one distinct workflow within COD, is the ability to create an event both as a node as well as a product which can be sold via the shopping cart. There are several other workflows though, and this is by no means the most important, as it is only just one feature.

7.4.1   COD Features

As we mentioned earlier, a feature is a set of functionality on a Drupal COD site. The features list can be accessed on *Administer>Site Building>Features* from the Administrative Panel (Figure 7.8).

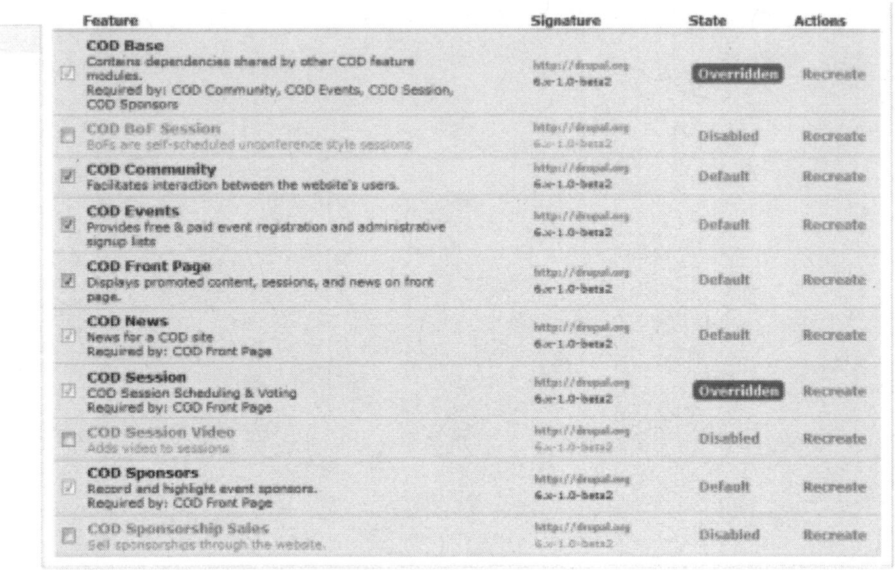

Figure 7.8   Features administration page

Features may be enabled by selecting the checkboxes and clicking the Save configuration button. Changing the configuration of the feature will cause the State to be shown as *overridden* or *needs review*; otherwise it will show as *default*, indicating that the configuration has not been changed. If you click on the State, link for any of the features, you will see more details about the feature and its components.

7.5   Content management

Content management is about creating new content. The image shown below tells us what is considered or permitted as content in COD (Figure 7.9). From this panel, we should see that apart from the default Page content type, the others are created by COD.

7.5.1   Creating an event

Conferences are usually comprised of multiple events. Yet, a daylong conference can be made up of multiple sessions, each of which is an event. Notwithstanding it is also possible to create a conference that consists of only one event, such as a music concert.

As we discussed earlier, an event in COD is both a node as well as a store product. Creating a node of the Event content type (node/add/event)

Figure 7.9   Content types panel

will display a form, which requires you to enter the SKU for you product. In e-commerce context, SKU refers to stock-keeping unit – which is a number or code that is used to identify each unique product or item available for sale in a store or in other business. The SKU for each event must be unique and will become the event's primary database key.

If you intend to charge money for your events, you will need to install and configure an Ubercart payment gateway. If this not your aim, you may completely disable Ubercart on the Modules admin page without any loss in other functionality for COD (Figure 7.10).

7.5.2   Sponsor setup

The COD sponsors feature is enabled by default and so also the Conference administration' admin menu. There are five sponsorship levels (Platinum, Gold, Silver, Bronze, Media) enabled by default which can be modified in the Sponsorship dropdown list of the Sponsor content type at admin/content/nodetype/sponsor/fields/field_sponsorship_level.

When you open the form to create a sponsor, it should look like Figure 7.11.

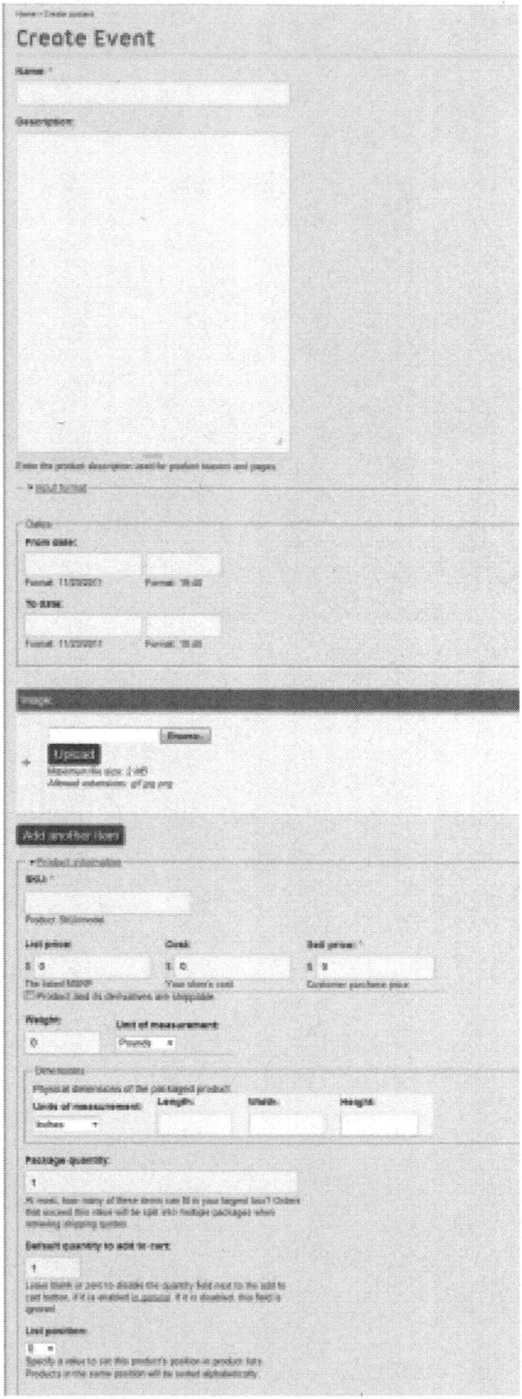

Figure 7.10 Event node creation form

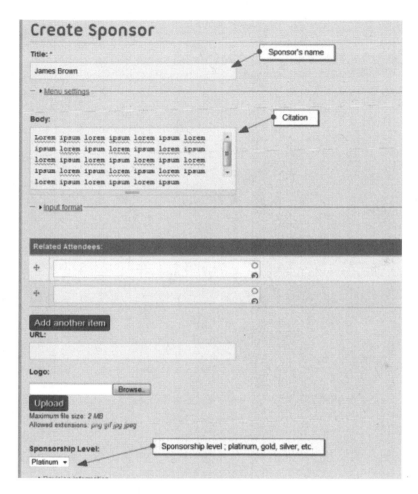

Figure 7.11   Sponsor node creation form

If you want to permit sponsors to create their own sponsor node or page, you will need to change permissions to affect this. Displaying sponsors is done on the Blocks view level. There are separate sponsor blocks for the home page and internal pages, and sponsor blocks can be moved into any desired block region.

7.5.3   Creating a room

A room is the place where an event is likely to take place. It must have a title or a description as well as an indication of the capacity. The purpose of this is to inform planners about the number of attendees the room must contain (Figure 7.12).

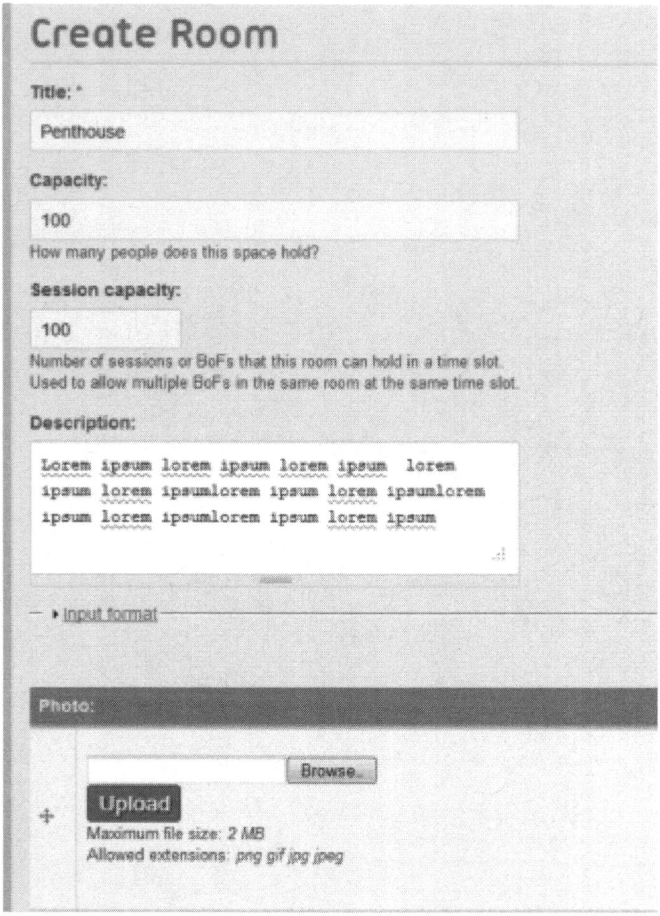

Figure 7.12   Room node creation form

7.5.4   Create session

What is a session? It may be one event or a group of events running consecutively in the same room. For example, a daylong conference may have two sessions conveniently named Morning Session and Afternoon Session which are separated by a Lunch Break. Typically, the Morning and Afternoon sessions will also have a Coffee Break. The form for creating a session will look something like Figure 7.13.

Note though that Sessions cannot be created without first creating Time Slots for the sessions.

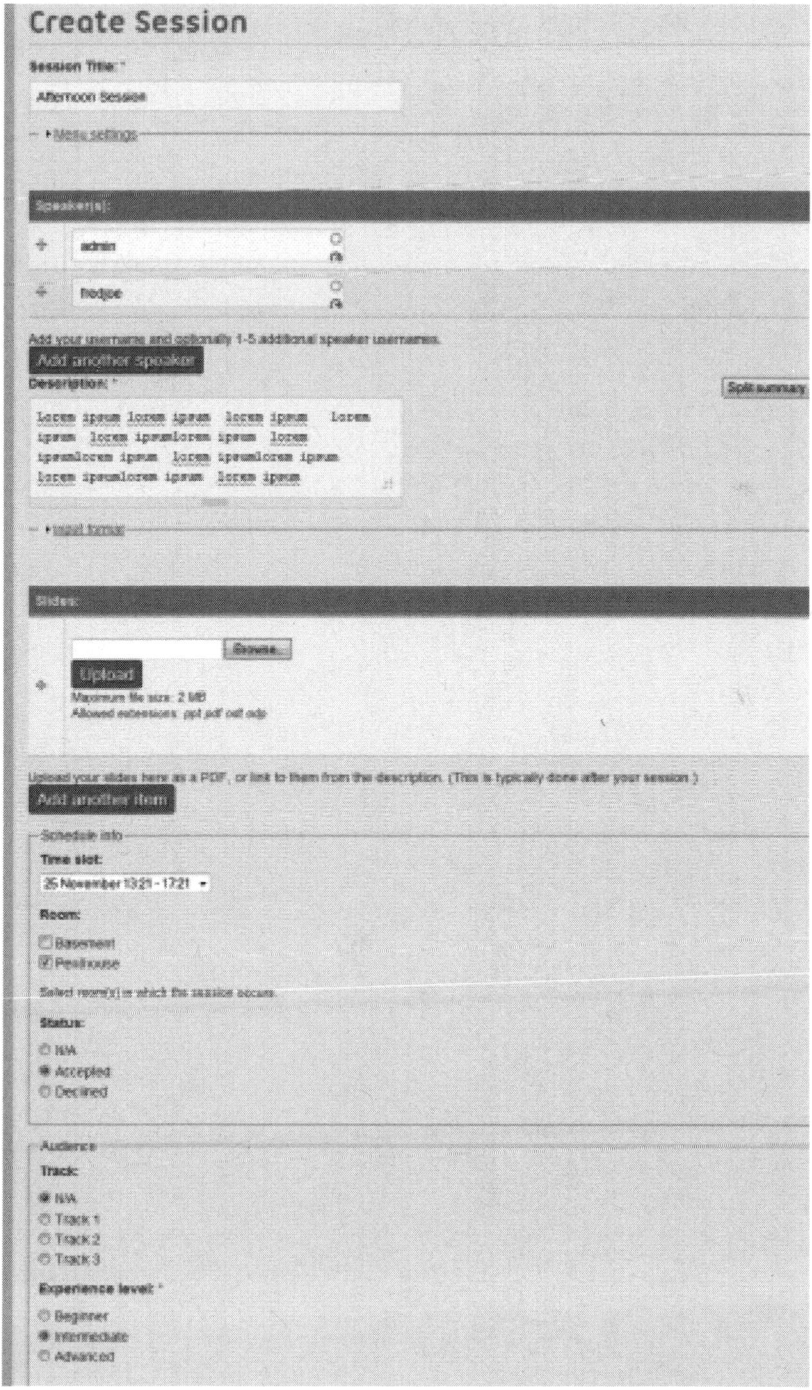

Figure 7.13   Session creation form

On closer look, we shall see that each Session is actually just another event, in the definition term though rather than as a content type, since it has a defined start and a finish.

7.5.5   Creating the schedule

The COD schedule view doesn't display anything until rooms and time slots have been created, and sessions are assigned to time slots. Sessions and Schedule items are different content types. A Schedule item is something like a Lunch break that doesn't have a presenter or track, but needs to be assigned a room and time slot.

Note that both Sessions and Schedule items need to have a Room and Time slot assigned to them to appear in the schedule. They must also have been Accepted and Published by the site administrator. Again, it is not possible to schedule two sessions/schedule items in the same time slot and room (Figure 7.14).

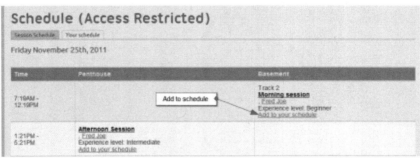

Figure 7.14   Schedule administration

7.5.6   Create product

Distinct from an Event node, a separate Product type node is defined by COD. This will often be used to create tangible physical items which may be purchased at the conference, such as videos, books, gifts, etc. The submission form for this type of node isn't any different from the Event node creation form. Thus, it seems the importance of this content type is to make it easy to create different shopping cart catalogs for tangible and non-tangible conference items (Figure 7.15).

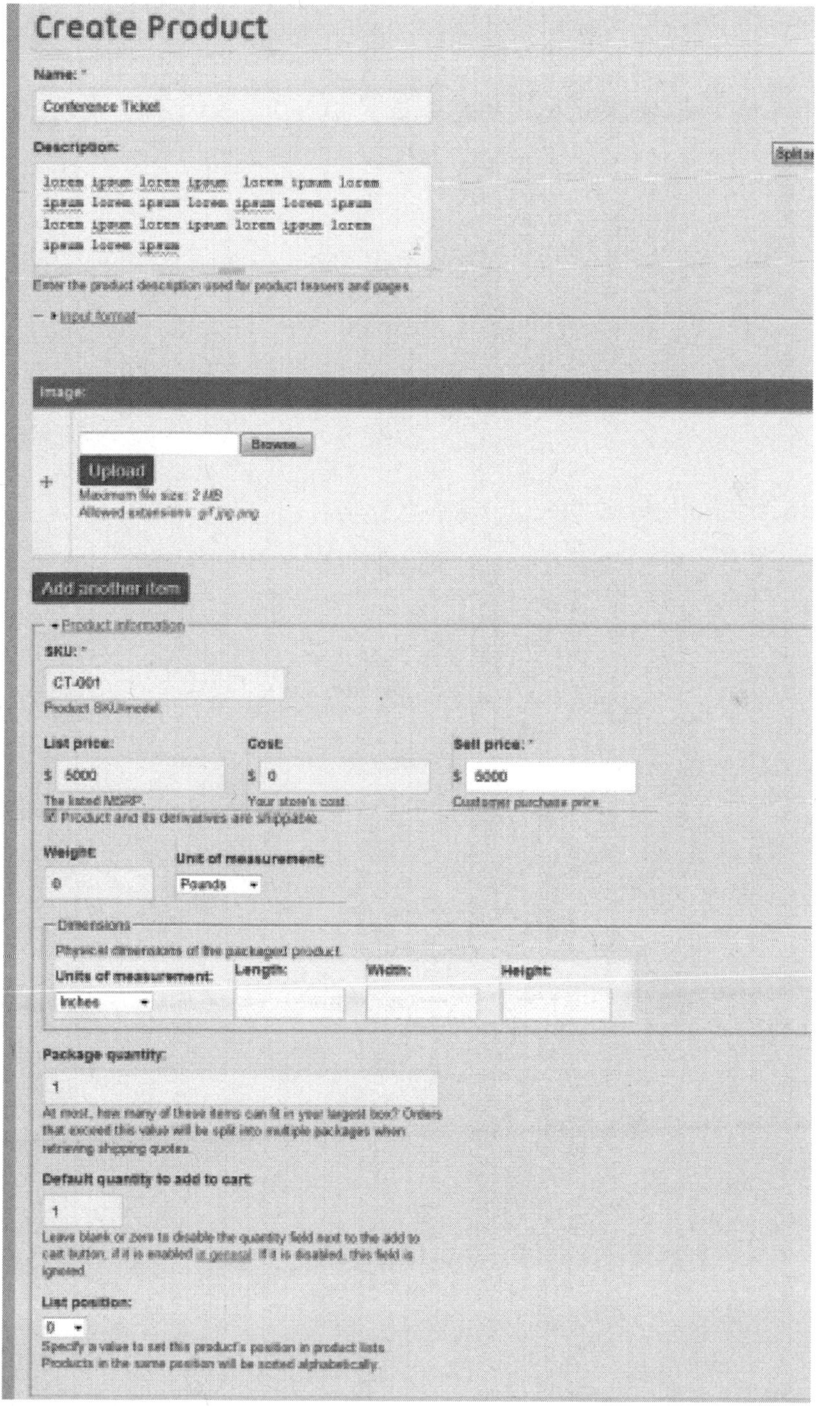

Create Product

Name: *

Conference Ticket

Description:

Split a

```
lorem ipsum lorem ipsum  lorem ipsum lorem
ipsum lorem ipsum lorem ipsum lorem ipsum
lorem ipsum lorem ipsum lorem ipsum lorem
ipsum lorem ipsum
```

Enter the product description used for product teasers and pages.

— ▸ Input format

Image:

Browse...

+ Upload

Maximum file size: 2 MB
Allowed extensions: gif jpg png

Add another item

— ▾ Product information

SKU: *

CT-001

Product SKU/model.

List price:	**Cost:**	**Sell price:** *
$ 5000	$ 0	$ 5000
The listed MSRP.	Your store's cost	Customer purchase price

☒ Product and its derivatives are shippable

Weight: **Unit of measurement:**

0   Pounds   ▾

— Dimensions —

Physical dimensions of the packaged product.

Units of measurement:	**Length:**	**Width:**	**Height:**
Inches ▾			

Package quantity:

1

At most, how many of these items can fit in your largest box? Orders
that exceed this value will be split into multiple packages when
retrieving shipping quotes.

Default quantity to add to cart:

1

Leave blank or zero to disable the quantity field next to the add to
cart button, if it is enabled in general. If it is disabled, this field is
ignored.

List position:

0   ▾

Specify a value to set this product's position in product lists.
Products in the same position will be sorted alphabetically.

Figure 7.15   Product node creation form

7.6   Administering COD

Having learned how to create the content we can look in brief at how to make them work together. We shall be looking at basic administration of the COD site, as well as how to create a community functionality for attendees.

7.6.1   Creating conference attendees

The first registered user on a new Drupal site is the Admin user, and by default the user who has absolute permissions on the site and may create other users and assign them into roles. By default on a COD site, people can make themselves members of the site, without administrator oversight.

7.6.1.1   Attendee profiles

User accounts contain personal information. First and last names are required because they are displayed on the community page, and for presenters, their full name will be displayed on schedules and session nodes. Organization name, job title and interests are optional. You can also modify or create additional fields at /admin/user/profile.

7.6.1.2   Add free signups

No one is considered an attendee until they have paid for their ticket. In some cases however, the organizers may want to give away free tickets, especially for keynote speakers, sponsors, organizers or other volunteers. Only users with *administer user* and *administer signup* permissions can do this.

- If a user account does not exist for the attendee, you need to create the account.
- Signups are executed on the event node. Go to the event node and click Signup and then click add to create a signup (Figure 7.16).
- Enter the username of the attendee, and click Sign up
- This user is now a registered attendee and should immediately receive an email notification.

7.6.2   Creating a community for attendees

Full names of attendees as well as core profile fields are displayed and filterable by clicking the community tab at the top of the site. If attendees have

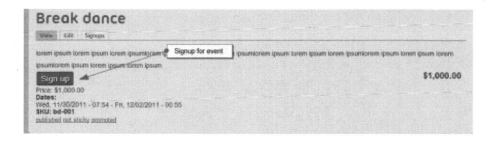

Figure 7.16   Sign up for event

been permitted to upload their photos, the photos will appear on the site. Only people who have signed up for the event will appear in this list.

The COD community feature is enabled by default. On this page, users may search for other attendees by name, company, or interest.

7.6.3   Administering schedules

Schedules can be viewed from the Session schedule tab at the top of the site. This view is restricted by default, it doesn't display anything until rooms and time slots have been created, and sessions are assigned to time slots.

7.6.3.1   BoF scheduling

Birds-of-a-feather (BOFs) type sessions are those sessions where there is very little moderation and the persons submitting content decide the scheduling. For example, in a Drupal conference this could be a discussion group on a subject such as Drupal e-commerce. If BOF is permitted, the feature will have to be enabled on the admin/build/features page. Permissions will also need to be granted to a role to schedule BOF session content and to create, edit and own BOF sessions.

7.6.3.2   Multiple BOFs in the same room

It may be possible to hold multiple BOF sessions in the same room. However, you need to make sure you have time slots and rooms available. If you visit the BOF schedule page at programs/BOFs, the links to add BOFs will be visible.

BOF scheduling is relevant for conferences hosting several hundred or perhaps thousands of attendees. It will not be discussed in detail in this book.

7.7   Conference management

Common conference management tasks (e.g. session moderation) appear in the Admin module menu as follows (Figure 7.17).

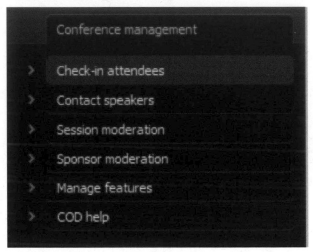

Figure 7.17   Conference administration side panel

7.7.1   Session collection

The COD Session feature and the Conference administration admin menu are enabled by default. As sessions are created, the administrator will have to visit the Session administration page (conference-admin/sessions) to manage the sessions, review and publish submitted sessions so they can be made visible to the public (Figure 7.18).

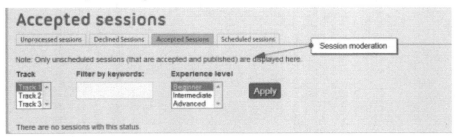

Figure 7.18   Session administration

7.7.2   Voting on sessions

To enable votes to be fairly applied, voting usually begins only after you've finished accepting new sessions. You need to adjust flag access on the Session vote flag, in order to allow other roles to vote on sessions. This should be removed when you want to stop allowing people to vote (Figure 7.19).

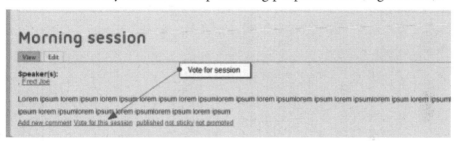

Figure 7.19   Voting sessions

7.7.3   Your Schedule display

After sessions have been decided, and you're ready to allow people to add sessions to their personal schedule, go to admin/build/flags page and edit the session schedule flag to assign access to this flag for all the roles you want to give this privilege. You can also add this flag to additional schedulable content types; such as workshops (Figure 7.20).

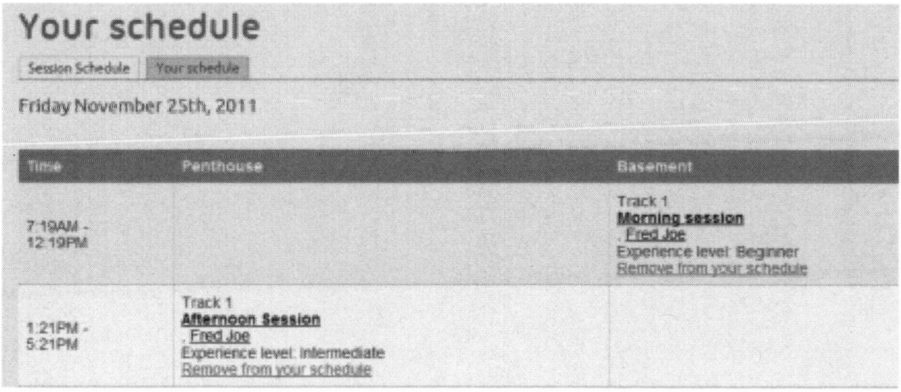

Figure 7.20   Schedule display page

7.7.4   Checking in attendees

In the conference management menu you will find a *Check in attendees* link. This will take you to the conference admin/checkin page. This page lists everybody who has a signup ID, together with their full name, username, signup time and more. When attendees arrive to collect their badge and other materials, simply click a checkbox next to their name and click *Mark signup attended*. Only a site user with the Attendee Manager role can conduct this operation.

7.8   Building COD Skills

There are so many other ways to customize a COD site, and only the basics have been dealt with in this book. However, these basics are more than sufficient to implement the installation and management of a conference site of moderate complexity. Additional training to help the user build knowledge and administrative skills is available from Acquia, who offers classroom style courses that can meet these needs. More information can be obtained from the Acquia web site.

7.8.1   Other online resources

- Conference Organizing Distribution documentation:http://drupal.org/documentation/build/cod
- Creating sessions and a schedule: http://usecod.com/screencast/creating-sessions-and-schedule
- DrupalCamp and Event Organizing Guide: http://groups.drupal.org/node/136494

7.9   Summary

This chapter shows how to create a conference site with the Drupal COD distribution. It shows how to install the software and takes the user through the basic configuration. The chapter identifies the salient features of an installed COD site and shows how to administer the features to create a functional and effective conference management framework. It concludes with showing where users can get more advice and assistance on how to carry out more advanced administrative tasks on a COD site.

Chapter 8

Creating a News Publishing Site with OpenPublish

Newspapers and magazines often need to put their content online either to widen their readership base or to create more revenue. Many have created elaborate blogs and maintenance-heavy static sites to fill this need. However, most have come to the realization that, a well-designed newspaper site will go a long way towards fulfilling these objectives.

- Permit readers to comment on content and actively engage readership into becoming part of the content creation process
- Integrate the online publication with social media platforms
- Widen readership and increase monetization opportunities with the internet.

8.1 Acquia OpenPublish

OpenPublish is a packaged distribution of Drupal created for online publishing. This distribution is intended for users of a variety of media outlet sites including newspapers, journals, online magazines, trade publications, broadcast, wire services, and membership publications. OpenPublish can run on most environments configured to run Drupal.

8.1.1 Benefits

Several features of OpenPublish support activities such as the following:

- Basic news coverage
- Web 2.0 trends
- Social publishing
- Semantic tagging
- Topic hubs

All the components of the OpenPublish distribution, which are mostly Drupal core and contribution modules are well documented, supported and modularly designed.

8.2   Installation

In general, the current release of OpenPublish should work with the same general system requirements that you will use for Drupal 6. However, during installation, issues relating to memory requirements are common. Therefore, the installation environment for OpenPublish should have the following as a minimum configuration:

- Memory_limit variable, in php.ini needs to be at least 128MB. The developers recommend 220MB.
- Sometime the installation presents a white screen of death or errors preventing completion. In this case try setting:
  - max_execution_time to around 120 seconds
  - realpath_cache_size to 512KB, 1MB or even 2MB
  - max_input_time to around 120 seconds

8.2.1   Obtaining your download

The free download may be obtained in both .tar and .zip formats from the OpenPublish website http://openpublishapp.com/download. The project details, together with the issue queue can also be viewed on the Drupal site http://openpublishapp.com/doc/download-openpublish.

8.2.2   Completing the installation

Installing OpenPublish is similar to installing Drupal 6. The OpenPublish setup walks the administrator through an installation wizard. Once the installation is launched from a web browser, you will see a familiar Drupal setup screen (Figure 8.1).

After selecting your preferred language , continue the setup by entering the database information as you would in a typical Drupal installation. If you are familiar with installing Drupal, you will notice that the OpenPublish installation takes a bit longer than the standard Drupal install. This is to be expected since OpenPublish packages many additional modules on top of the core Drupal bundle. At the completion of the installation process, the result should look like following (Figure 8.2):

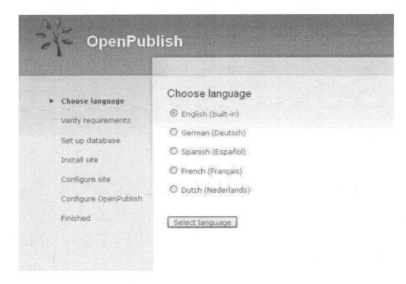

Figure 8.1   The installation setup screen

Figure 8.2   The installation completion screen

8.3   Configuration

An intuitive user interface in OpenPublish provides several administration pages that allow the configuration and management of site content. This interface is available to the individual who installed the site (administrator), The privilege to use the interface can also be given by the administrator to other roles.

8.3.1   Accessing administration page

A user with administrative privileges will see a wrench icon in the upper-left corner of publicly facing pages, such as the front page (Figure 8.3).

Figure 8.3   The administration toolbar access icon

If this wrench is clicked, it will reveal the OpenPublish Admin Toolbar which looks like the following (Figure 8.4):

Figure 8.4   The administration side toolbar

There are three main tabs in this Admin Toolbar, which should be of interest to an administrator, the others being more relevant to a site developer. These three tabs have the following labels:

- **Create content**. Clicking on this tab will reveal other tabs that may be used to create content such as new pages, blog posts, articles, etc.
- **Devel.** This tab gives access to functions relevant to the site developer. Most site users and administrators may never have to use this tab.
- **Administer.** The child tabs under this tab are relevant to the overall administration of the site. These tabs link to administrative functions which are grouped according to related purposes.

8.3.2   Changing the site logo

The site logo can be changed using the same process as a Drupal 6 site. To do this, navigate to Administer>Site Building>Themes. Select Configure on the current default theme, upload the new logo, and save the configuration.

8.3.3   Features

OpenPublish comes with several features, some of which may not be required on your news publishing site, and can be disabled. In addition, too many features tend to make a site run slower. You may see a list of the enabled features on the Administer>Site building>Features page (Figure 8.5).

8.4   Content Management

Content management refers to the creation, organization, and modification of content. Content management on an OpenPublish site is quite similar to a Drupal 6 site. However, OpenPublish provides several additional features that are described in the following sections.

8.4.1   Taxonomy

Several vocabularies come with OpenPublish by default. For example, the *Topic* vocabulary includes terms like *Business, Health, Politics,* and *Technology.* Some of these also contain child terms. For example, the *Politics* term also has child terms listed as *Local, National,* and *International.* These are

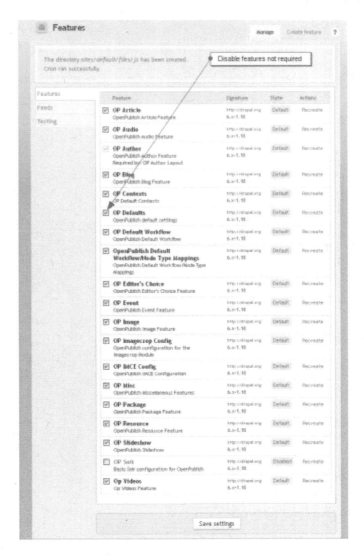

Figure 8.5   The Features administration page

displayed in the main menu. Clicking on them will show a list of content items tagged with that term.

8.4.1.1   Managing vocabularies

Vocabularies may be conveniently accessed and modified through the Admin toolbar. To do this click on the Administer tab and navigate to Administer>Content management>Taxonomy. This will show the Taxonomy page (Figure 8.6).

Figure 8.6   The taxonomy administration page

To add another vocabulary click on the *Add vocabulary* tab at the top right corner of the Taxonomy page (Figure 8.7).

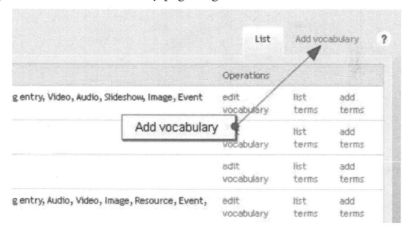

Figure 8.7   Creating new vocabularies

This will show a form, which will prompt you to define a new vocabulary (Figure 8.8).

- Enter the *Vocabulary Name*
- Enter a *Description* for the vocabulary
- Select the content types which may be tagged with terms from this vocabulary

Figure 8.8   Defining the new vocabulary

■ You may choose to enable *Tags*, which effectively allows users to supply their own terms during the process of creating content. Otherwise, leave this disabled if you want a strictly controlled or hierarchical vocabulary.

■ You may choose to enable *Multiple* select and allow users to apply multiple terms from the new vocabulary you have created to content they create.

■ If you enable *Required* this will force users to select at least one term from the new vocabulary when they create a content item.

8.4.2   Create content

A very detailed User Manual for site administrators and users can be found at the OpenPublish site. However, this sections provides a description of how to manage a few of the many features of this framework.

To create a new node, click on the *Create content* tab in the Admin Toolbar (Figure 8.9). This will show a full list of the different content types you can use to create a node. These include *Article, Audio, Author, Blog entry, Editor's Choice, Event, Image, Package, Page, Panel, Resource, Slideshow, Topic Hub,* and *Video*.

For example, clicking on the *Article* tab will show the following content creation form (Figure 8.10).

Many of the fields on this form are straightforward and what we are already used to. These are fields such as:

■ Title
■ Body
■ Teaser

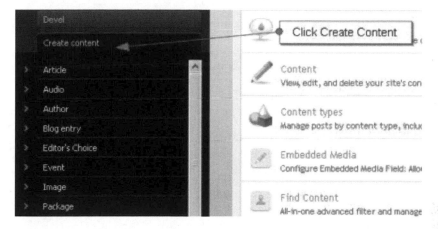

Figure 8.9   Creating new content

Figure 8.10   The content creation form

However, the Article creation form contains several custom fields, such as the taxonomy, image and file upload fields.

8.4.2.1   Using taxonomy to categorize content

There is always the option to categorize content on the *Vocabularies* section of the content creation form if taxonomies have been created and linked to that content type. In this case, the vocabulary topic has been linked to the Article content type and therefore shows under the Vocabularies section of the form. From the dropdown list, select the Topic and select the term that best describes the content you are posting (Figure 8.11).

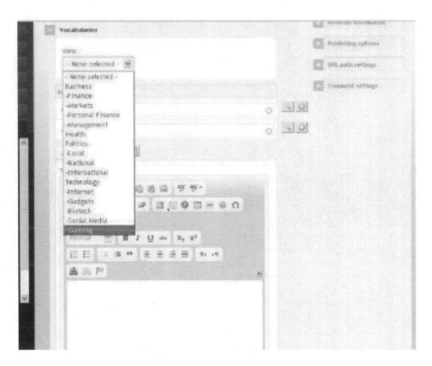

Figure 8.11   Selecting taxonomy terms for content

8.4.2.2   Creating a deck

A deck is a small headline that runs below the title and doubles as the main headline in an article. It is also called a Drop Head (Figure 8.12).

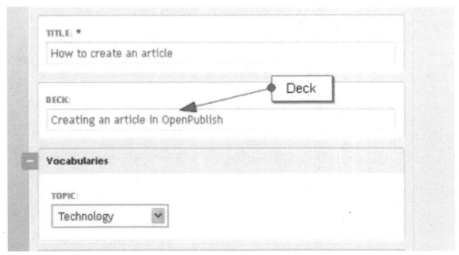

Figure 8.12   Creating a deck

8.4.3   Adding files

In the *File attachments* section, it is possible to upload files with several permitted extensions such as jpg, jpeg, gif, png, txt, doc, xls, pdf, ppt, pps, odt, ods, and odp. To upload a file, click the browse button to find the file on your local computer, and then upload it to the web server by clicking the attach button (Figure 8.13).

When checked, the *List* checkbox will list all uploaded file attachments below the article so readers can view or upload them. The URLs of all uploaded files are also displayed to make it easier for them to be referenced in the body field or elsewhere in the site.

File attachments

Changes made to the attachments are not permanent until you save this post. The first "listed" file will be included in RSS feeds.

ATTACH NEW FILE:

C:\Documents and | Browse...

Attach

Figure 8.13   Adding files to content

8.4.4   Adding images

There are three ways to add images to your posted content.

1.   Upload from your computer through *File attachments* upload
2.   Browse from files already uploaded into your website
3.   Reference the image as a remote URL

For a main image of the article, it is best to upload the image through the Main Image upload button. This automatically renders and styles the image at the top of the article (Figure 8.14).

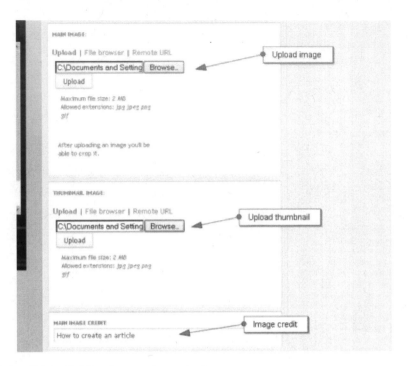

Figure 8.14   Adding images to content

8.4.5   Adding multimedia

OpenPublish supports the inclusion of multimedia elements in content. Audio, video and image content can be easily uploaded or embedded in the site from third-party sites.

8.4.5.1   Audio

OpenPublish natively provides an audio content type. This is suitable for storing media locally on your site or by referencing 3rd party providers. You will be able to add an audio node the same way as you would any other node although the node creation forms are slightly different. To do this, go to *Create Content=>Audio* in the Admin menu (Figure 8.15). You will be presented with two ways to add audio:

- **By embedding.** You may post external code from custom URLs for remote mp3 files. or third party providers such as:
  - Odeo: http://www.odeo.com/
  - Podcast Alley: http://www.podcastalley.com
  - podOmatic: http://www.podomatic.com

When you enter the URL or Embedded Code, the embedded third party content will be consequently parsed and appropriately displayed.

- **By uploading.** You may upload mp3 audio clips from your local machine.

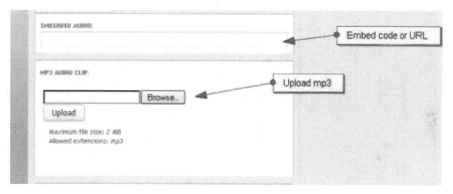

Figure 8.15   Adding audio as content

8.4.5.2   Video

Uploading video is done in about the same manner as uploading audio. To add a video node, go to *Create Content>Video* from the Admin menu. There are three ways to add video.

- **By embedding.** You may post external code from third party providers such include The following services are provided:
  - Archive.org: http://www.archive.org
  - Blip.tv: http://blip.tv
  - Dailymotion: http://www.dailymotion.com
  - Google: http://video.google.com
  - GUBA: http://www.guba.com
  - IMEEM: http://www.imeem.com
  - Last.fm: http://www.lastfm.com
  - Live Video: http://www.livevideo.com
  - MetaCafe: http://www.metacafe.com
  - MySpace: http://vids.myspace.com
  - Revver: http://one.revver.com
  - Sevenload: http://www.sevenloads.com
  - Spike TV: http://www.spike.com
  - Tudou: http://www.tudou.com

- Twistage: http://www.twistage.com
- UStream.TV: http://www.ustream.tv
- Vimeo: http://www.vimeo.com
- VoiceThread: http://www.voicethreads.com
- Yahoo! Music: http://new.music.yahoo.com
- YouTube: http://youtube.com
- **Custom URL.** When you enter the URL or Embed Code, the embedded third party content will be parsed and displayed appropriately.
- **By uploading Flash.** You may upload .flv video clips from your local machine, if you decide to host your own video files.

8.4.5.3   Images

Uploading images is done in about the same manner as uploading audio and video content. The same content creation functionality applies to images in terms of support for both local and remote content. To add an image node, go to *Create Content>Image* in the Admin menu. There are two ways to add image content.

- **By embedding.** You may post external code from third party providers such include Picasa, Photobucket, ImageShack, Flickr and custom URLs. When you enter the URL or embed code, the embedded third party content will be parsed and displayed appropriately.
- **By uploading.** The Main Image field is a standard file field where you can upload the image you want to associate to this node.

8.4.6   Editing Content

There are two ways to edit content that already exists on a site. With the first method, find the node you want to edit, and then click the Edit tab on the Admin Toolbar (Figure 8.16). This will enable you to edit any field in the content being viewed.

When you are finished making your changes, click the Save button to conclude the edit.

The second method of editing is designed for a situation where there are many nodes on the site and you need to hunt for a particular node to edit. In this case; navigate to *Administer>Content Management>Find Content* on the Admin menu (Figure 8.17).

Figure 8.16   Editing content from node view

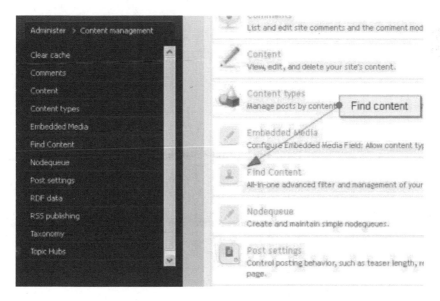

Figure 8.17   Accessing the content filter page

There are several ways to find existing content with the Find Content tool and these options are presented with radio buttons that are displayed to indicate searchable fields (Figure 8.18).

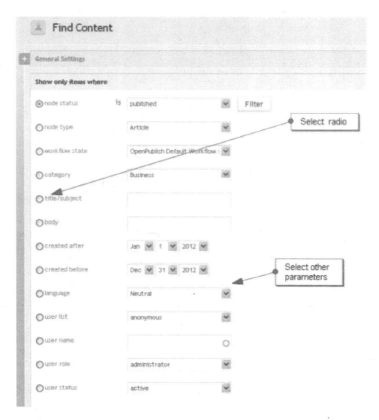

Figure 8.18   The content filter page

An example of searching for existing article content should include the following:

- Select the Node Type radio button. In this case, we will filter by: *Article*, then select *Filter* and the search results will display articles.
- Select the title/subject radio button and enter a search word in the title of or body of the content, then select filter.

8.5   Other Features

There are several other features of OpenPublish, and some will be briefly discussed here because although they are not as critical as others they do improve the content and display of the site.

8.5.1   CKEditor

CKeditor is a WYSIWYG editor. It is a tool like a word processor which should help you generate HTML in a What You See is What You Get fashion. The layout of the functionality is intuitive and should be easily understandable for anyone already used to word processors (Figure 8.19).

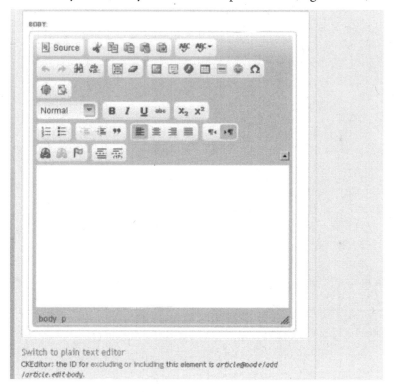

Figure 8.19   CKeditor user interface

8.5.2   Calais

Calais is a web service provided by Thomson Reuters. This service will analyze a node and automatically identify and extract semantic metadata/tags from the content of a node.

The web service also identifies related facts, events, and more. For example, if Microsoft is mentioned in your content, this service will perform contextual analysis to determine if the content is more about Microsoft than any other terms which have been identified. Calais requires a key from http://www.opencalais.com/APIkey to function.

8.5.3   Related terms

Related Terms are displayed in OpenPublish and include a list of the Calais terms that were applied to that node. When you click on a term, this will reveal a list of Articles tagged with that term.

8.5.4   More Like This

The More Like This modules enable the display of related content from your site or from around the web on your node pages by using the Calais terms that are most relevant.

8.5.5   Topic Hub

Topic Hubs harness the power of Calais tagging, to create associations based on one or more of a site's most commonly used tags. The display may be of views/blocks, like most commented stories, most read content for the topic, most active contributors, and links to other related topics. Integration with Calais Geo allows the plotting of the content of a specific Topic Hub on a map. Here's an example from Governing.com (Figure 8.20):

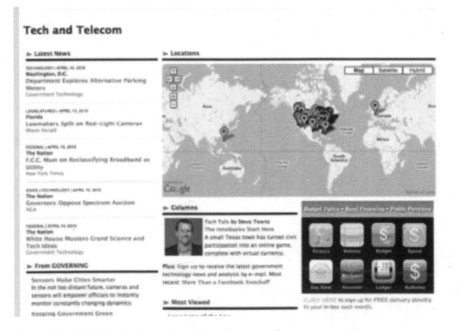

Figure 8.20   Topic hub content plotted on a map

8.6   Improving OpenPublish skills

A well-illustrated though slightly dated manual for users and administrators may be found at the OpenPublish web site. Also, Acquia, the developer of the OpenPublish distribution, organizes skill development training for various categories of users.

8.7   Summary

This chapter shows how to create a news publishing site with the Drupal OpenPublish distribution. It shows how to obtain and install OpenPublish, and takes the user through the basic configuration. The chapter identifies the important features of an installed OpenPublish site and shows how to administer the site to create a functional and effective news publishing framework. It concludes with showing where users can get more advice and also assistance on how to carry out more advanced administrative tasks on the OpenPublish site.

Chapter 9

Creating an Intranet with Open Atrium

An intranet typically facilitates communication between people or work-groups to improve the knowledge base of an organization's employees. In its simplest form, an intranet consists of an internal email system and maybe a message board service. Intranets that are more sophisticated may include internal web sites, a database and a document management system.

Although it may not be easy to justify the cost of creating and main-taining an intranet, in easily quantifiable terms, the advantage is quite appreciable especially in a large organization with staff occupying a large premise or spread out over large geographical areas. A few of the advantages of a corporate intranet are enumerated as follows:

- Improvement in workforce productivity by helping users locate and view information faster
- Time savings by enabling organizations to distribute information to employees on an as-needed basis
- Improved communication by enabling communication of strategic initiatives that have a global reach throughout the organization
- Cost effective maintenance and access to documents such as requisition forms, procedure manuals, and internal phone directories.
- Enhance teamwork by allowing information to be easily accessible by all authorized users.
- Easily integrated information accessed through standards compliant web browsers which are available for use across several platforms (Windows, Mac, UNIX, etc.). This also allows the intranet to be linked to a company's management information system, for example a time keeping system.

9.1   Open Atrium

Open Atrium is an open source intranet framework which comes with six features; a blog, wiki, to-do list, Shoutbox, calendar, and a dashboard for managing these features and for adding new ones. The framework also features group spaces to allow interaction between users with the same interests. Open Atrium is built on the Drupal framework.

9.2   Installation

The process of installing Atrium is very similar to installing Drupal. In general, the current release of Open Atrium should work with the same general system requirements that you will use for Drupal 6. The following server side configurations are suggested for installing Open Atrium.

- PHP 5.2.x and greater
- PHP GD extension
- 64MB memory
- MySQL 5.0.41+
- Apache with the mod_rewrite module for clean urls (required for imagecache, profile picture support, etc.) or
- Nginx, using clean urls with php-fpm

Additionally, on the browser end Open Atrium has been tested to support the following:

- Firefox 2+
- Safari 3+
- Internet Explorer 7+

Atrium does not support Internet Explorer 6 or browsers with JavaScript disabled.

9.2.1   Obtaining your download

Obtain the free download of Open Atrium in both tar and zip formats from the Open Atrium website (http://openatrium.com/download). To find out more about Open Atrium project details go to http://openatrium.com/ community web site.

9.2.2   Completing the installation

Installing Open Atrium is similar to installing Drupal 6. In the initial setup screen, select the Open Atrium profile.

Figure 9.1   Initial setup screen

As usual, you would begin the setup by entering the database information. At the completion of installation, the result should look like following (Figure 9.2):

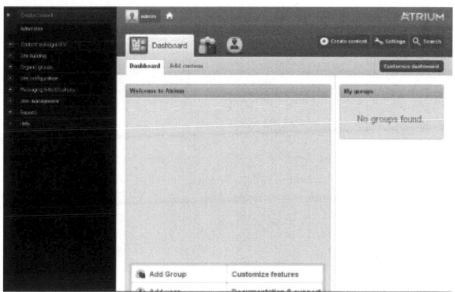

Figure 9.2   Installation complete front page

9.3   Configuration

The administration dashboard of Open atrium provides an intuitive user interface for the management of site content and configuration. By default, it is immediately available to the user who conducted the installation of the site.

9.3.1   Accessing administration page

A user with administrator privileges will be able to see a wrench icon in the upper-left corner of all of the site pages, such as the front page (Figure 9.3).

Figure 9.3   Administration panel access icon

When this wrench is clicked it opens up a side panel which contains the Open Atrium Administration Toolbar with links to the various administrative features of Open Atrium (Figure 9.4).

9.3.2   Changing the site logo

One of the most important tasks that the administrator will do is change the Open Atrium logo to that of the organization. If you click the Customize Features tab after completing the installation, you will be presented with a page where you can enable main site features and specify a default front page. If you click the images tab, you be able to upload a new logo (Figure 9.5).

Otherwise, the site logo can be changed as you would with a Drupal 6 site by navigating to Administer>Site Building>Themes. Select Configure on the current default theme page and upload the new logo, then save the configuration.

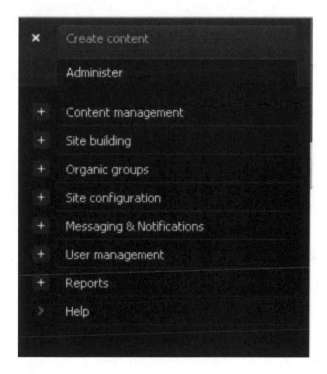

Figure 9.4   Administration toolbar

9.3.3   Features

Open Atrium comes with an overwhelming list of administrative features. For the new user it may be advisable to choose only the most critical of the many user features that are also available. Any administrator who is familiar with administering a Drupal site should be able to navigate the administrative back end.

A list of the enabled features can be found on the Features page. This page is located at Administer>Site Building>Features. There are two main classes of features which are relevant for basic use. These are the Atrium and the user-related optional Features. The features listed under these options are as follows:

9.3.3.1   Atrium

This class contains core features which include:

- **Atrium**. Atrium site wide settings and configuration

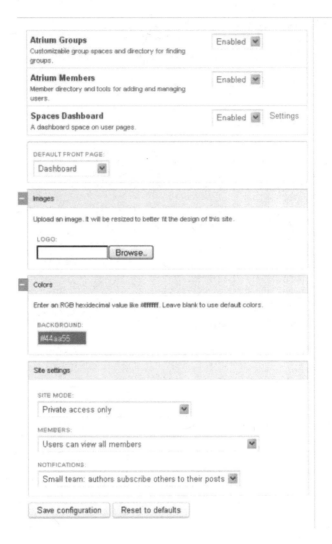

Figure 9.5   Basic settings

- **Atrium Groups.** Customizable group spaces and directories for finding groups
- **Atrium Members.** Member directory and tools for adding and managing users
- **Atrium Profile.** A personal profile to share information about yourself with your team

9.3.3.2   Features

This class contains the optional features which are listed as follows (Figure 9.6):

- **Atrium Activity.** Activity streams for showing new posts, updates and comments.
- **Atrium Blog.** The blog lets you have a conversation on a topic with your team.
- **Atrium Notebook.** The notebook feature lets you store and share information and attachments.
- **Atrium Calendar.** The calendar lets you share events and meetings with your team.
- **Atrium Case Tracker.** The Case Tracker lets you assign tasks to yourself and others and track the progress on a project.
- **Atrium Reader.** The reader lets your share news, images and twitter feeds with your team.
- **Atrium Shoutbox.** The Shoutbox provides a team microblog.
- **Spaces Dashboard.** A dashboard space on user pages.

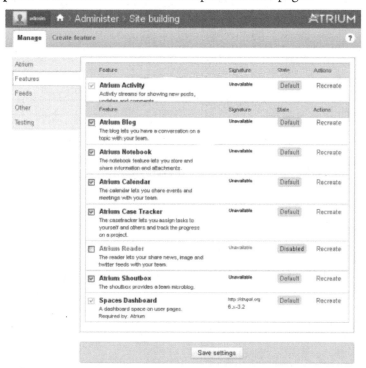

Figure 9.6   Features administration page

9.3.3.3   Adding new features

A new feature can be added by clicking on the Create Feature tab at the top of this page. This will be a task for advanced Drupal users and will not be discussed here.

9.4   Creating a new admin user

In some circles, the person who has created a Drupal site is known as the "God-user" simply because they would have absolute permissions and the power to do almost anything to the configuration, content and other users on the site, including the power to create a new user (Figure 9.7). If it is a big and busy site with many users, he/she might indeed need to create some other administrative users to be able to delegate the responsibility for general day to day maintenance.

The project developers for Atrium recommend that such a user create a new administrative account and to only use the creator account (also known as user/1) for such matters as site configuration and database maintenance.

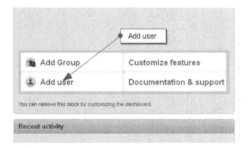

Figure 9.7   Creating a new user

To create a new administrative user, go to the front page and click on the Add User button. This will bring up a form which looks like following (Figure 9.8):

You only need to fill in some basic information to add a new user on this form. Save the form after completing. You may then log out of the *God User* account and log in under the newly created administrator account.

9.5   Creating groups

Groups are the building blocks of the Open Atrium intranet framework. Activities occur in groups and they enable users and discussions to be

Figure 9.8   Adding a new administrator

organized into meaningful collections. Users can belong to multiple groups. Any user who is part of a group can typically participate in that group's discussions and receive new and updated post notifications.

We will create an example group for persons concerned with any aspect of finance in our organization to participate in ongoing discussions and we will call this group *Finance*.

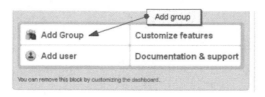

Figure 9.9   Adding a new group

To create this group we click the Add Group button on the front page (Figure 9.9). This will bring up the following form (Figure 9.10).

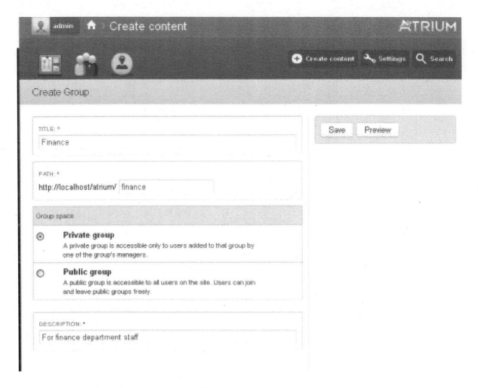

Figure 9.10   Creating group details

The same may also be achieved by clicking the groups' icon in the main navigation pane. This will display a directory of groups on the site. The Add Group button can be found on the top right of this page.

After creating the group, you will be directed to the to the group dashboard (Figure 9.11), where content and users may be added and managed.

Figure 9.11   Group dashboard

9.6   Creating users

Now that we have created a group, let's try and add some committee members to it. To do this, click the user icon in the main navigation pane to go to the Members area (Figure 9.12):

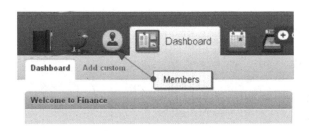

Figure 9.12   Adding users to group

Here we will find a list of all the members that belong to the Finance group. The creator of a group is automatically added as a member, so the Admin creator is also listed. There are two ways of adding a user: either by adding an existing user, or creating a new Atrium user (Figure 9.13).

Figure 9.13   Group users directory

- To add a new user, click on the Add user button to bring up a form like the one we used previously to create a new admin user.
- To add an existing user, simply type their username in the small box on the right and click the Add to group button.

Thereafter, if you click the *Directory* tab in the sub-navigation menu, as shown in Figure 9.13, you'll see the new user listed with the other group members.

9.7   Creating content

Open Atrium has the Notebook and Blog features enabled by default. For most people familiar with Drupal, the Notebook functions in the same way as the Book content type. It is useful for organizing multi-page content, where each page reads like a new chapter or section. The blog feature is also similar to Drupal—running commentaries by one or several users, with or without comments below them.

9.7.1   Adding new content type

Other content types are native to Atrium but need to be enabled. These include Case and Event. To turn this on you will have to enable them in the Features page in Administer>Site Building>Features.

New content types are created in the same way as you would on a Drupal 6 site; go to the Content Type page at Administer>Content management>Content Type, and select Add content type at the top of the page.

9.7.2   Adding a blog entry

The blog feature provides a means of sharing stories and information with other members of a group. To add a blog entry click on the Create content tab in the upper right-hand corner and select Blog entry. This has to be done while in a Group space, else the only content type option presented will be Group (Figure 9.14).

Figure 9.14   Creating blog posts into groups

After filling in the post, you may select who will receive notifications for the post. Any member that selected to receive notifications will also be sent e-mail notifications for updates to the post while they are subscribed. A list of the blog posts for a group can be displayed by clicking the Blog icon at the top of the page (Figure 9.15).

Figure 9.15   Posted blog entry

9.7.3   Adding a book

With the Notebook feature, you can manage and share documents and attachments within a group. This feature is from within the group dashboard. A Notebook may contain several books with each book containing one or more book pages, of which each one is a separate web page which can be retrieved and edited.

To create a new book, click on the Notebook icon at the top of the page, then click on the Add book page button at top right. You will see that the Book Outline section has no other reference than Create a new book (Figure 9.16).

After saving the book, click the Add book Page button to add a new page where you can select the top book page as the Parent page. In a single book you are allowed no more than nine child pages (Figure 9.17).

9.7.4   Add Event

Adding events in a group is made possible by the Calendar feature of Open Atrium. Click on the Create content button in the Navigation menu and select Event to add an event from anywhere in your group. Alternately, click

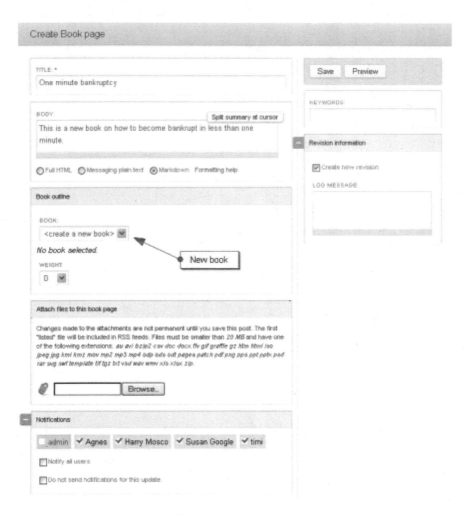

Figure 9.16   Creating a new book page

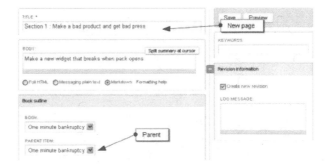

Figure 9.17   Book page creation form

the Add event button while on any calendar page. This will bring up a form like following (Figure 9.18):

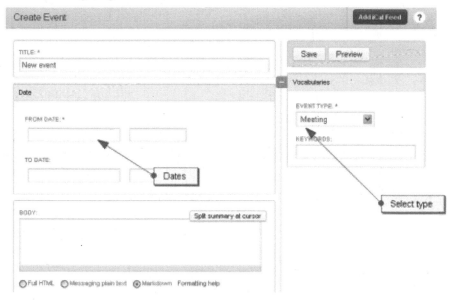

Figure 9.18   Creating an event

To complete this event form, select a From date, and optionally a To date from a drop-down display. All other inputs are standard. There are four possible event types to add as default event types. These can be added to or edited on the Taxonomy page Administer>Content Management>Taxonomy. After doing this, click the Save button. The main calendar page looks like this (Figure 9.19):

9.7.5   Add case

The Case Tracker and the Blog features allow for discussion through comments. However, the difference between the two is that a case tracker case represents an issue that needs to be solved, whereas a blog entry is more like information shared for the mere purpose of an open-ended discussion. The Case Tracker is a full ticketing system which enables the assignment of to do lists and the creation of unlimited projects within each group on the intranet. The case tracker also enables the classification, prioritization, and management of the status of each project.

Cases are classified under projects. Group managers can add new projects by clicking the Add Project button.

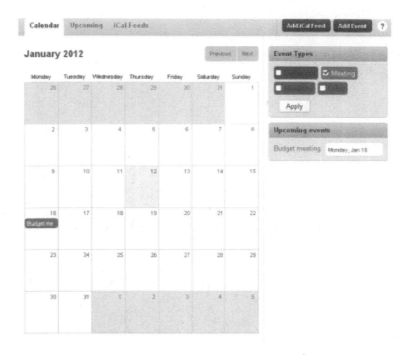

Figure 9.19   Event calendar

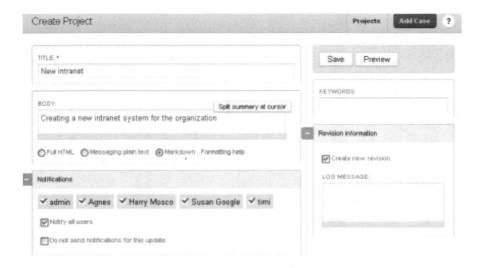

Figure 9.20   Creating a project

Fill in a title for your project (Figure 9.20). Optionally, you can add a description, configure notifications for your project, and attach files. When you are done, click Save.

Cases are "to do" items for a project. They represent tasks that can be assigned to users, given a status and a priority ranking. Group members can add a new case by going to the group homepage and clicking Case Tracker>Add Case, or by clicking the Add Case button while on a project page (Figure 9.21).

Figure 9.21   Creating a case

A case will typically contain the following information (Figure 9.22).

- **Project.** Defines the project this case should belong to
- **Assign to.** Defines the individual in the group who is responsible for this task
- **Status.** Cases can be Open, Deferred, Resolved, Duplicate, or Closed. If a case is Closed, Duplicate or Resolved it is automatically removed from active case listings.
- **Priority.** Priority can be Low, Normal or High
- **Type.** What type is the case? Bug, Feature request or General task?

Figure 9.22   Typical case

9.7.6   Create Shoutbox

The Shoutbox is a private micro blogging service not unlike Twitter. It enabled users in a group to share short messages, links, and information. However, it must be enabled on the Features page of the site for it to work. Shoutbox can be viewed by clicking the bird icon in the top navigation area. This will display an overlay with the last several shouts, as well an input box to add a new one. Clicking the full view link at the bottom of the overlay will show a full page view (Figure 9.23).

To create a shout, type your text or provide a link in the text area and click on the Shout button. This will display your new shout at the top in both the dashboard view as well as on the Shoutbox overview page.

9.8   Working with the dashboard

The Dashboard enables monitoring activities within a group or space. Within the Dashboard you can also customize blocks that contain information from other sites, such as widgets and feeds.

Three sets of dashboards are possible; the site home page, groups, and users. A group dashboard is the group's home page. You can access it by clicking on the Groups tab and selecting a group. Your user dashboard can accessed by clicking on the user icon and selecting Dashboard. Both dashboards have similar functionality (Figure 9.24).

Figure 9.23   Using the Shoutbox

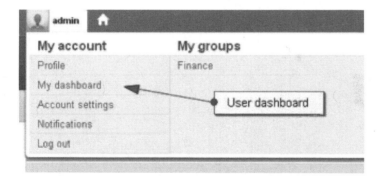

Figure 9.24   User dashboard

You can add new blocks to a dashboard. You can also add up to five dashboards per space. To add a block to the dashboard, click the Customize dashboard button at the top right of the page. This will open up an overlay that contains dialog boxes from which you can select new blocks (Figure 9.25).

9.8.1   Section (1) Layout selection.

The options available include three layouts:

■   **Default**. Main content area with a smaller column to the right

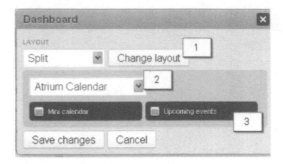

Figure 9.25   Customizing the dashboard

- **Columns**. Three equally sized columns
- **Split**. Two equally sized columns

9.8.2   Section (2) Category selection

This section contains a drop-down for the category of the block.

9.8.3   Section (3) – available blocks

This section shows the blocks available in the category selected in section 2. If nothing shows in Section 3, it means there are no blocks available for the selected category.

To add a block, just drag the box from section 3 to the dashboard page and position it where you want it to appear. If it is a valid block position, you will see a box with a dashed outline and you can drop the block inside this box. When you have dropped the block, its content will be displayed on the dashboard. To make the change permanent, click the Save changes button in the overlay (Figure 9.26).

9.8.4   Available blocks

The following is a list of the blocks available by default from the dashboard overlay. If any of these blocks exist in the dashboard, they will not appear as an option in the overlay.

9.8.4.1   Atrium

- **Welcome (for admins).** A video introducing admins to the tools available to them, and a few helpful administrative links

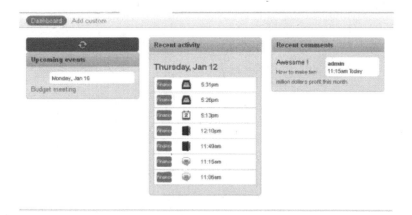

Figure 9.26   Customized dashboard

- **Welcome (for members).** A video introducing site users to Open Atrium
- **Recent activity.** Displays recent activity in the group or user space, including new content and comments
- **Latest files.** Displays a short list of the latest files uploaded to the site.

9.8.4.2   Atrium Blog

- **Blog teaser.** Displays a short list that includes teasers for the latest blog posts together with a link to the contributing user
- **Recent comments.** Displays a short list of the most recent comments on blog posts

9.8.4.3   Atrium Calendar

- **Mini calendar.** This block contains a small calendar with events marked out as colored lines.
- **Upcoming events.** This block contains a short list of upcoming calendar events.

9.8.4.4   Atrium Case Tracker

- **My cases.** The block features a list of Case Tracker cases assigned to the currently logged in user
- **Latest cases.** Features a list of the most recently added Case Tracker cases
- **Projects.** Contains a list of Case Tracker projects

9.8.4.5   Atrium Groups

- **My groups.** Displays a list of the groups that the current user belongs to

9.8.4.6   Boxes

- **Add a custom box.** This block enables a user to add a block which they can fill in with their own content

9.9   Developing Skills

Open Atrium comes with many available features especially on the administration back end. Skilled users of Drupal 6 may be able to navigate without too much problem. Some detailed user instructions are available at the Atrium web site. The project developers may also be able to offer tuition or installation assistance. Inquiry information may be found at http://ww.openatrium.com. You can also find some basic help notes at the Atrium site help pages (http://yoursite/admin/help).

9.10   Summary

An intranet facilitates communication between people or work groups to improve the knowledge base of an organization's employees. It would typically consist of an internal email system, a message board service, internal web sites, a database, and a document management system.

This chapter shows how to create an intranet site with the Drupal Open Atrium distribution. It shows how to install the software and takes the user through the basic configuration. The chapter identifies the important features of the installed Open Atrium site and shows how to administer them to create a functional and effective intranet framework.

Chapter 10

Creating a Learning Management System with ELMS

A Learning Management System (LMS) provides a means of putting educational instruction in a form that makes it more accessible to a large group of users at all times. This method of delivering instruction is useful to educational institutions for course delivery as well as corporate organizations for staff training and evaluation. It will generally be of benefit to institutions and organizations with target audiences spread out over a wide geographical area.

Apart from enabling users to learn at their own pace, an LMS could drastically cut the cost of training since attendance at a physical location can be eliminated or reduced. Some other reason an LMS could be a useful tool for instructional purposes include the following:

- Immediate access to training on 24/7 basis throughout the year
- Reduced delivery costs per course due to self-paced learning
- Greater consistency in training

10.1 ELMS

ELMS (e-Learning Management System) is a completely open source project built on the Drupal Content Management System. It was originally developed at Pennsylvania State University, College of Arts and Architecture e-Learning Institute. ELM aims to reduce technical barriers for instructional designers and faculty through the use of outlining and page creation tools.

10.1.1 Benefits

Since it has been built for instructional designers by instructional designers, ELMS could be useful for rapid assembly of e-learning materials through easy to use tools and interfaces. Here are just some of the benefits of the ELMS platform.

- Ability to integrate with central learning systems
- Rapid prototyping of courses
- Course content is separate from course communication and course design
- Developed around sound instructional design principles
- Open source and built on the Drupal 6 platform
- Schedule builder to streamline course communication process
- Ability for students and staff to bookmark their progress

10.2   Installation

Installation is not different from installing a Drupal 6 web site. You need to download the ELMS distribution from http://drupal.psu.edu/fserver and unzip to your server. After doing this, go to the ELMS folder on your server from a web-browser as you would when installing Drupal. Once the installation is launched from a web-browser, you will see the familiar Drupal setup screen (Figure 10.1).

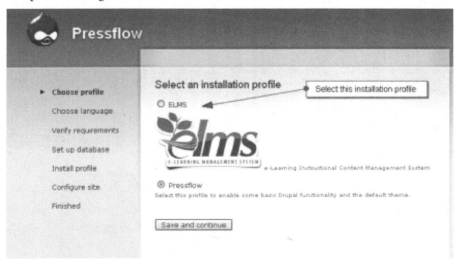

Figure 10.1   Installation setup screen

Pressflow profile is the default selection when the setup screen appears. Select the ELMS installation profile option instead and run through the installation. Begin the setup by entering the database information for the site. If you are familiar with installing Drupal, you should have no problem installing ELMS. When the installation is complete, the front page of the site should look like the following (Figure 10.2).

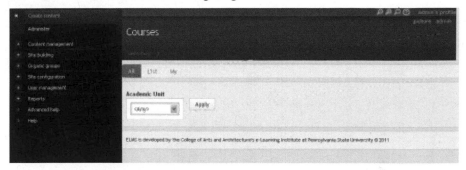

Figure 10.2   Installation complete front page

Note that the default front page is titled "Courses" which should progressively list all the courses available for use on this portal. If you wish to change this default, you can do this by going to Admin>Site Configurations>Site Information or http://yoursite/?q=admin/settings/site-information.

10.2.1 Possible installation problems

Some server related problems might arise during the installation. These could include the following:

- **White screen.** This is often due to inadequate provisioning of resources and occurs mostly on localhost installations. A way to get around this problem is to increase two settings.

    1. The *php_value* memory limit to a minimum of 128M in the *.htaccess* file, or by removing the line completely. Otherwise, increase this limit directly in the *php.ini* file.

    2. The maximum time for scripts to a value higher than 60 seconds in the *php.ini* file.

- **MySQL packet error.** This also occurs mostly in localhost installations or on a shared server, and it is usually due to the view caching process. A possible solution is to run the following command at the mysql console: "*set global max_allowed_packet = 10 * 1024 * 1024.*"

10.2.2   Page Not found

CleanURL is enabled by default during installation. On the localhost and other servers which do not support CleanURL, this may present a problem because every link from the front page will give a Page Not Found error. A way around this is to locate the CleanURL page in the Administration dashboard by entering following link in your browser: http://yoursite/?q=admin/settings/clean-urls. Here you can turn the feature off (Figure 10.3).

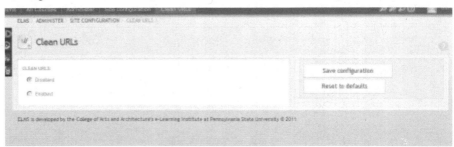

Figure 10.3   Enabling cleanURL

10.3   Configuration

Like in all Drupal installations, an intuitive user interface in ELMS provides several administration pages that allow the management of the site's content and configuration. As usual, this interface is enabled by default available to the first user—the developer/administrator who conducted the installation of the site. The privilege to use the interface can be given by the Administrator to other roles.

10.3.1   Accessing administration page

A user with administrator privileges will be able to see a wrench icon in the bottom left corner of public facing site pages, such as the front page (Figure 10.4).

If this wrench is clicked, it will reveal the ELMS Admin Toolbar which looks like the following (Figure 10.5):

There are two main tabs on the Admin toolbar: Create Content and Administer. The Create Content tab will be visible to all permitted roles reveals other tabs that are used to create content—principally new courses, and new course spaces.

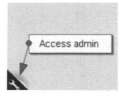

Figure 10.4   Administration panel access icon

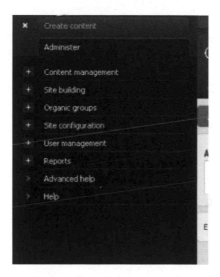

Figure 10.5   Administration panel

The Administer tab should mainly be of interest to an administrator. The child tabs under this tab are relevant to the overall administration of the site. These tabs link to administrative functions.

10.3.2   Terminology

The following terminologies will be encountered while learning to use ELMS.

- **Course space.** A Course Space is used for the reservation of name space in the system and primarily helps to organize course versions. Alone, it serves no other function than to publish the fact that a course exists.
- **Course version.** A Course Version an the organizational unit which allows you to implement and offer a course. Versions are

described by different stages of course development such as *archived, sandbox* and *offered to students.*

- **Outline designer.** This is the course outline and editing interface used for the rapid creation and modification of course outlines.
- **Templates.** Like themes, these are reusable page components that have been previously created and are recommended as good starting points for the creation of any page. More templates can be easily added.
- **Course content.** This feature bundles everything together related to the online creation and management of the course content.

10.3.3   Roles

The basic installation of ELMS comes with eight defined user roles with varying privileges as follows.

- Anonymous user
- Authenticated user
- Administrator
- Instructional designer
- Instructor
- Staff
- Student
- Teaching assistant

This list can be edited and additional roles can be added by going to Admin>user roles or the http://yoursite/?q=admin/user/roles page (Figure 10.6).

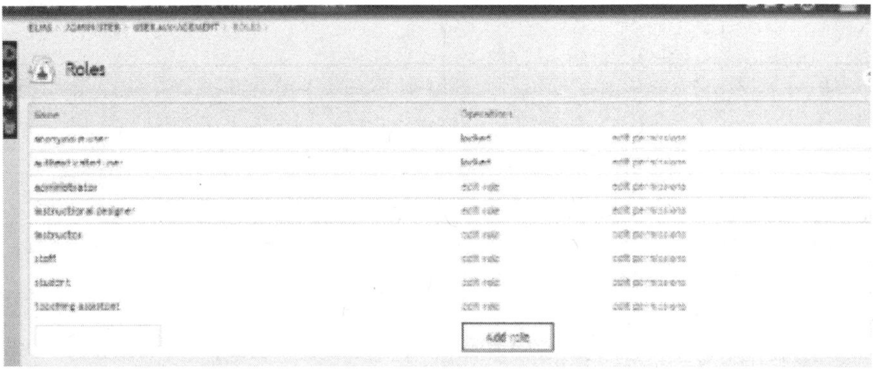

Figure 10.6   Administering roles

10.3.4   Changing the site logo

The default theme of ELMS is the Rubik theme which does not have a logo position. If you have used a theme that permits uploading a logo, the logo can be changed as you would the logo from a Drupal 6 site. To do this, navigate to Administer>Site Building>Themes, or the http://yoursite/?q=admin/build/themes web page. Select Configure on the current default theme page, upload the new logo, and save the configuration.

10.3.5   Features

ELMS comes with several features which are ready to use and some that are still in the development stage but are included in the distribution. The most important of the currently functional core features are (Figure 10.7):

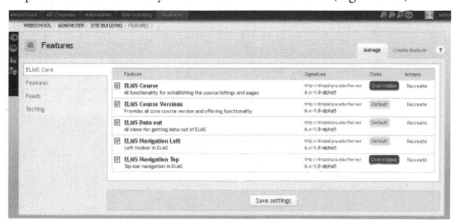

Figure 10.7   Core features

There are also optional features that are important; else the ELMS functionality may not be wholly available. These include the following (Figure 10.8):

10.3.5.1   ELMS Instructional Content

This is the backbone of instructional design and content development for ELMS. It is installed by default with ELMS and includes an easy to use site outlining tool known as Outline Designer.

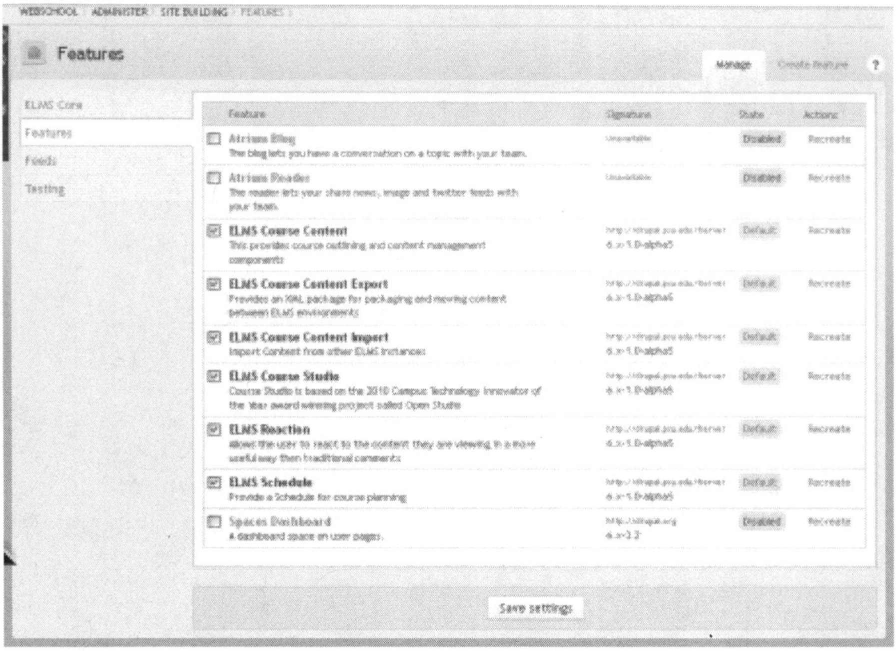

Figure 10.8   Administering optional features

10.3.5.2   Spaces

Spaces in ELMS is no different than Spaces in an Intranet (covered in the preceding chapter) and will not be described here. However, the primary function of Spaces is to provide configurable, full-featured organic groups or course versions.

10.3.6   Content management

Content management refers to the creation, organization, and modification of content on the site. Content management on an ELMS site is similar to a Drupal 6 site. However, there is related functionality on an ELMS site, which we discuss in the following sections.

10.3.6.1   Taxonomy

ELMS is installed with a single vocabulary called Academic Units. This also includes four neutrally titled terms which are [Department 1, Department 2...].

Vocabularies can be accessed and modified through the Admin toolbar. To do this, click on the Administer tab and navigate to Administer>Content management>Taxonomy or the http://yoursite/?q=admin/content/taxonomy web page. This will show the Taxonomy page.

You may add and edit new vocabularies and terms in exactly the same way as you would on a Drupal 6 site. To add another vocabulary, click on the "Add vocabulary" tab at the top right corner of the Taxonomy page (Figure 10.9).

Figure 10.9   Administering taxonomy

10.3.7   Adding content

Some detailed video tutorials for site administrators and users can be found at the ELMS site. However, following is a description of how to manage a select few of the many features of this framework.

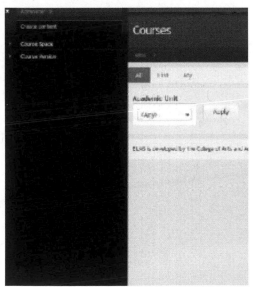

Figure 10.10   Creating content

In the following example, we will be creating a Space titled Technical and the adding to it a single Course Version titled Introduction to Elms.

10.3.7.1   Create a Space

A space will typically belong to an Academic Unit. Spaces work in roughly the same way as they do with creating an Intranet with Open Atrium (Figure 10.11).

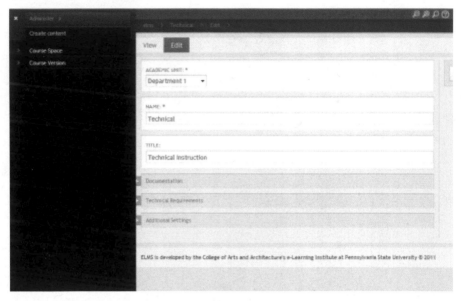

Figure 10.11   Creating a space

Here the entries are quite straightforward. Beyond the basic descriptions, you will have to make some other entries under the Documentation and the Technical Requirements tab. The Documentation tab will prompt you to:

- Upload syllabi and other sample materials to give students a feel for the course
- Upload documents that could help facilitate course communication between faculty members and instructional designers

The Technical Requirements tab will require that you select browsers and plugins supported in the course.

10.3.7.2 Create Course Content

To create a new Course version, click on the "Create content" tab in the Admin Toolbar. This will show a list of all the content types available in this view. If you have enabled the Space feature, you will be able to add the Course Version and Course Space. The Sandbox is used model your course before making it available for use (Figure 10.12).

Creating the main course description entry is a straightforward process. You need to enter the following self-descriptive parameters:

- Version name
- Course
- Description
- Instructional template—available as a dropdown selection
- Lessons—The number of lessons to start with

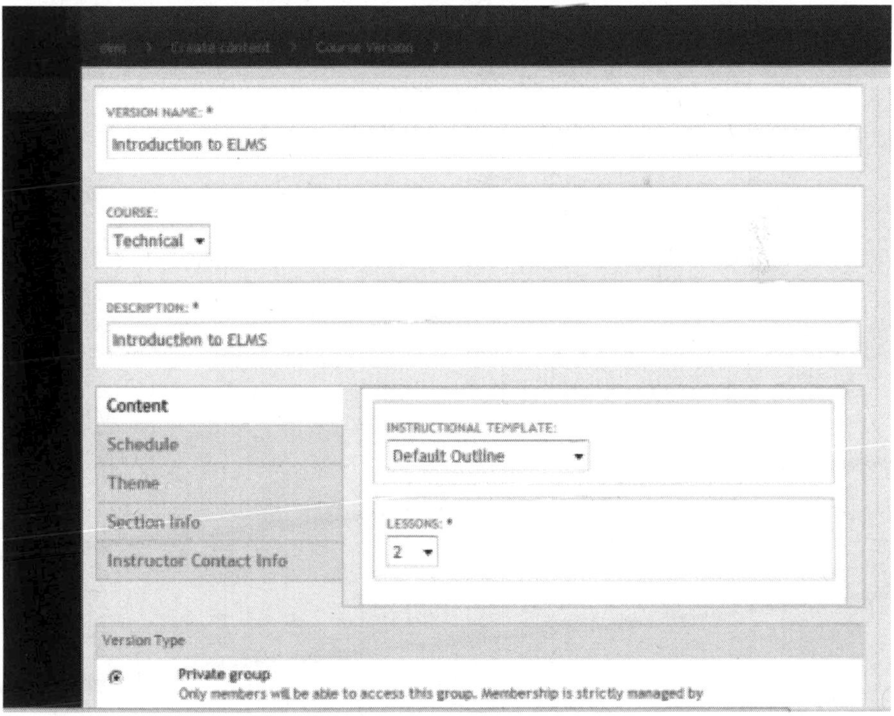

Figure 10.12 Creating new course content

The schedule tab (Figure 10.13) enables you to further describe the course version in more detail:

- **Scoring method.** This will base all Event Score values on points or percentages. Points is the default and this value won't be used unless you decide to add points to events.
- **Schedule to build.** Select if you would like to build a new schedule from scratch or use a template. In the case of rebuilding a schedule you can either rebuild the dates or the entire schedule.
- **Schedule source.** Connect to the registrar or use manual date entry to build the schedule.
- **Top level name.** The name of the largest structural item in the schedule for Topic Based outlines/schedules.
- **Number of topics.** How many topics would you like to build? This will be used to spread the weeks of instruction evenly. You can always add or remove topics after creation.
- **Forming week structure.** How do you want weeks to be populated in schedule creation? You can either define a structure, not build one, or build one based on a prototype lesson (requires that a course structure exists).
- **Semester.** What semester is this course space being developed for?
- **Year.** The year this course will be offered.

Figure 10.13   Course schedule

Actually, even though the foregoing (course space and course version) are the two principal content types used in ELMS, the following is a list of available content types:

- **Course event**. Use this to add an event/task/container to the course's schedule
- **Course space**. Use this to setup a course name space to group
- **Course version**. Version of a course either for new development, to be offered, or for promotional purposes
- **Folder**. A folder is a container that holds lesson material of non-textual nature.
- **Link**. Create a link to external content in course outlines
- **Page**. Create a page of content for use in course outlines
- **Reaction**. Add a reaction to a page to the site
- **Studio submission**. Submit a new item to the course studio

Some content types may only be created at the course content level. Even though the names are a little different, the output of most of the listed content types will be similar to other default content types in a typical Drupal site.

10.4   Improving ELMS Skills

The greatest asset of ELMS is the ease of use, both for the course designer and the students. However, a detailed video on how to use ELMS can be found on the ELMS site. Support is also available through the ELMS project page on the Drupal web site.

10.5   Summary

This chapter describes how to create an online learning management system with the e-Learning Management System (ELMS). It shows how to install the software and takes the user through the basic configuration. The chapter identifies the important features of an ELMS site and takes the reader through the basics of how to administer the features to create a functional ELMS framework. It concludes with showing where users can get more advice and assistance on how to carry out ongoing administrative tasks on the ELMS site.

Chapter 11

Monitoring, Optimizing and Analyzing a Drupal Site

It is often easier to build a web site than to keep it functioning and performing optimally. This is especially true if you have built a public site and it has lived up to your dreams and become hugely popular with thousands of users and visitors every day. However, on the internet, there is a price to pay for success, and the cost will be often be the strain which the traffic puts on the server resources.

In many other cases, the problem that may arise may not be with server resources, but with the application itself. Maybe so much functionality has been included that the site ends up running slow and soon becomes frustrating to use when traffic is high. Perhaps miscellaneous cranks have decided to target it for mischievous purposes. Therefore, it often makes sense to have a means of monitoring, optimizing, and analyzing your site's performance in order to ensure that it remains serviccable and popular. There are several reasons to do this:

- To be adequately informed about problems with the site and how to improve the user experience
- To enable predictive assessment of security flaws
- To enable ongoing assessment of user behavior and needs in order to streamline content delivery to meet the demands of users

11.1 Monitoring

Sever resources are crucial to a website. If inadequate, frequent crashes may be expected. Drupal includes functionality to help monitor and understand why your web application is eating up server resources. This helps you decide what to do to either stop or alleviate the problem. There are three major performance parameters that should be adequately monitored: logging and errors, reports and security.

11.1.1   Logging and errors

The Logging module enables the logging and recording of system events to the database. If it is enabled, you will find a link to the Logging and errors page in the Admin>Configuration>Development section. This page provides options for the display and logging of errors.

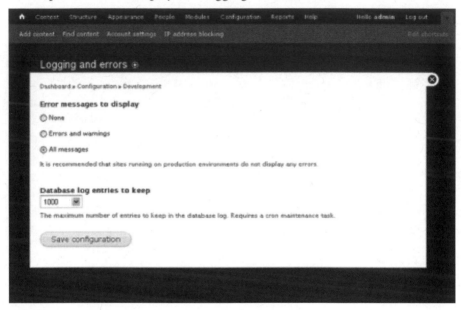

Figure 11.1   Logging and errors administration page

With the Error messages to display option, you can decide whether to write errors to the screen or not.

The All messages option, which is the default selection, is quite useful while you are in the process of building the site, as it enables you to progressively see what has gone wrong, where and when. The None option is for security reasons, and is preferable to use when you go live. This should prevent Drupal from publicly displaying information, such as database connection details, which malicious users may use to attack your site.

The Database log entries to keep setting, indicates the maximum number of messages to keep in the database log. This setting may put some strain on the database, and on some shared hosting sites where the database size is small, having too many records can cripple your site. Also, if Cron is not effective, the setting may not be observed and you find that the number of messages is not trimmed to the maximum that you have set. The error logs can be progressively checked in the Reports section of your site's Administration page.

11.1.2 Reports

Error messages and warnings are important indicators of the actual performance of the site and should help in maintaining a healthy website. Error messages will help you to isolate malicious attacks, users and programs that have attempted to access your site. By default, Drupal reports can provide some analytical information about your site users and their interests. The Reports page is accessed via the toolbar and the following basic links to the site's list of reports and logs are given:

Figure 11.2   Reports administration page

Enabling other modules such as the Syslog and Statistics modules in the Modules section, will provide additional reports as in shown in the following figure:

Selecting Recent log messages will show the site's log of recent events. Each of the log records display the type of record, its importance, who or what generated it, and the outcome of the event.

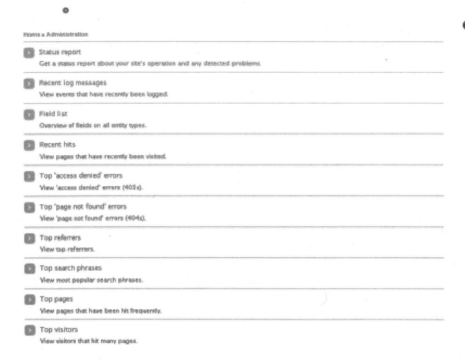

Figure 11.3   Reports page with syslog and statistics modules enabled

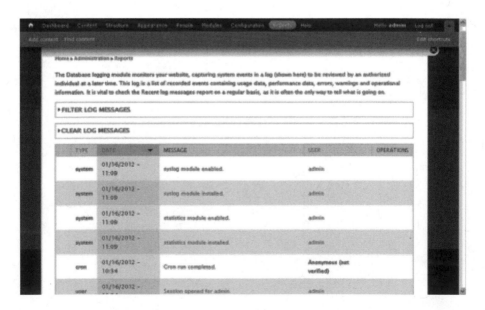

Figure 11.4   Event logging

In order to see the details of each message, click on the link found in the Message column. This will display the event detail in a screen such as following:

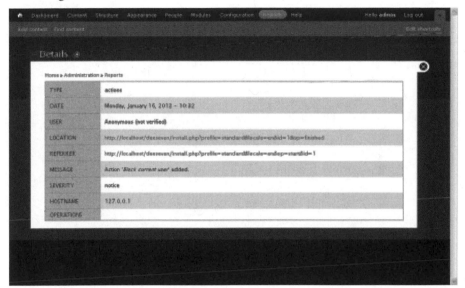

Figure 11.5   Typical event details page

There are several other pages that you should pay attention to in the Reports section. The most notable are the Status report and the Top access Denied Errors. The first, which is a report about your site's operation and any detected problems, will give you a summary of the site software and server details and warn of inadequacies. The latter will alert you of attempts by persons without permission to access the site. It could also alert you of unavailable or inaccessible requested resources.

11.1.3   Security

Drupal is an open source project, with unencrypted code, which means anyone with enough reason to, can look for potential security vulnerabilities. Thus, if your public site contains a lot of personal users' information that are not intended for public view, a hacker with sufficient motivation can harvest and use this information for illegal purpose. Therefore, it may be important to put some security in place to protect the application.

The Drupal web site has a section which is dedicated to security announcements, especially in relation to such matters as the latest security patches released. These security announcements can be found at http://drupal.org/security,

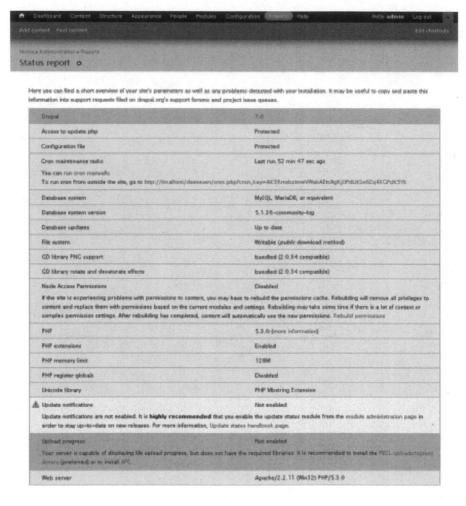

Figure 11.6   Status report page

or you may opt to receive such announcements via email or by subscribing to the RSS feed.

11.1.4   Security modules

However, there is a proactive role that site administrators need to play in ensuring the security of their site and the easiest way to do this is to install modules that will provide an active shield both for the control of access and the protection of data. The following are suggested modules.

11.1.4.1   CAPTCHA

CAPTCHA stands for Completely Automated Public Turing test to tell Computers and Humans Apart (CAPTCHA). This module will install a test which helps prevent malicious users using automated spam bots to sign up to your site.

11.1.4.2   reCAPTCHA

The reCAPTCHA module is an improvement and extension of the CAPTCHA module and it is similarly intended to frustrate automated submission by web bots, of web forms such as for registration, contact and content posting.

11.1.4.3   Mollom

This module if installed on a non-commercial website enables a free third-party service. It may be useful when an intelligent automated web bot has found ways to circumvent the CAPTCHA system. Mollom primarily works toward the prevention and discouragement of SPAM posting.

11.1.4.4   Legal

Sometimes it may be also prudent to protect yourself from future disagreement with site users regarding the use of content and other data they may have submitted. It may be wise to provide rules and policies, which users must read and accept before using the site. The contributed Legal module enables a terms and conditions box on the sign up form.

11.2   Optimizing

The purpose of optimizing the performance of your site should primarily be to improve users' experience. One of the greatest nightmares of site users is a site which runs sluggishly. Two functionalities which Drupal makes available to improve the working speed of a site are caching and bandwidth optimization. Both are accessible on the Performance page at Admin>Configuration>Development>Performance.

11.2.1   Caching

Every page request made from a Drupal website by a user makes a demand on the database, because that is where the data required to compile the page is retrieved. Caching is the process of storing copies of web pages in order to reduce the amount of effort required to repeatedly create a page. The

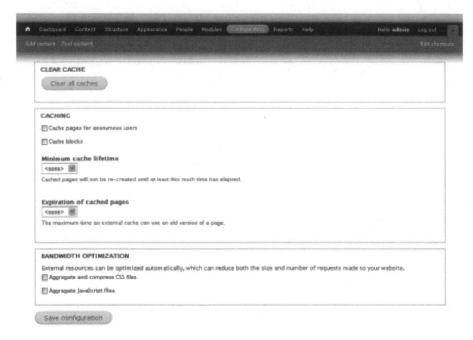

Figure 11.7   Performance administration page

caching functionality enables holding the most frequently requested pages in a cache, and thus making it unnecessary for calls to be made to the database every time these pages are requested. This can result in a great performance boom for highly trafficked sites.

- **Minimum cache lifetime and expiration of cached pages.** With these options, you set how long you want the cache to be held before it is refreshed. If you chose a long cache lifetime, Drupal will have less work to do compiling new content. However, it will also mean that it will take that long for new content to become visible on the site which may not be so good for a site where immediate user interaction is important. If for example, if your site is a daily blog, then the cache period may not matter a lot. However, if you have created a highly successful and interactive site like Facebook, you would clearly need a very low maximum cache time.
- **Block caching**. Blocks as we have learned are independently constructed from pages. They also make more elaborate database requests because of the way they communicate with the Drupal core. Drupal is also able to cache the content of blocks. If block

caching is enabled, blocks no longer have to query the database with every page refresh, thus Drupal has to do less work.

11.2.2 Bandwidth optimization

Most modules in a Drupal site come with their own styling components, defined in CSS and JavaScript files. Therefore, every time a demand is made of functionality, the module concerned often needs to separately load its styling data before it creates a display. It is possible for Drupal to aggregate and compress all the CSS and JavaScript files on a site in order to both reduce their total size and the number of requests made to a server.

The Bandwidth Optimization section on the performance page shows what options are possible.

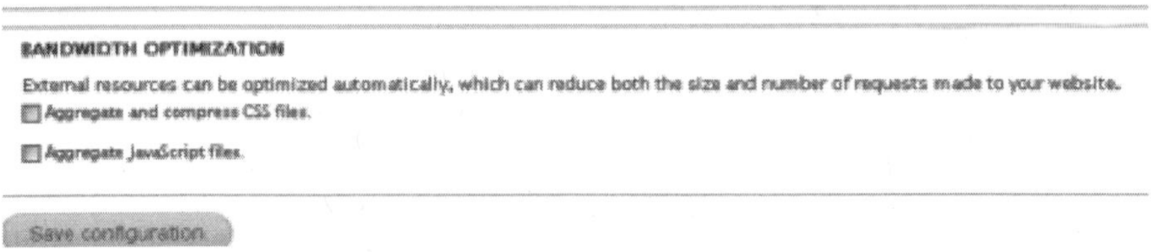

BANDWIDTH OPTIMIZATION

External resources can be optimized automatically, which can reduce both the size and number of requests made to your website.

☐ Aggregate and compress CSS files.

☐ Aggregate JavaScript files.

(Save configuration)

Figure 11.8   Bandwidth optimization

Files may not however be aggregated during development, because it interferes with work on theme development.

11.2.3 Performance Tips

Apart from caching, there are other tips which can be observed to make a Drupal site run optimally:

- **Disable unnecessary modules.** Enabled modules are loaded by Drupal and consulted anytime there is a page request. This unnecessarily consumes valuable resources.
- **Make sure Cron runs regularly.** If this is not done, some functionality may not work as intended.
- **Enable throttle.** The Throttle module enables Drupal to cut down on features to free resources in case of high traffic.
- **Video and audio performance.** Video and audio can tie up resources for a long time. If you need to use them on your site be aware of the consequences

- **Statistics module.** This and related modules tax the database and often it may be better to use an external analytics application.

11.2.4   Performance resource modules

There are some contributed modules which may appreciably improve the performance of your site. The following are worth looking at:

Advanced cache:	http://drupal.org/project/advcache
Authcache :	http://drupal.org/project/authcache
Block Cache Alter:	http://drupal.org/project/blockcache_alter
Boost:	http://drupal.org/project/boost
Cache browser:	http://drupal.org/project/cache_browser
CacheExclude:	http://drupal.org/project/cacheexclude
Cache Router:	http://drupal.org/project/cacherouter
CSS Gzip:	http://drupal.org/project/css_gzip
Javascript Aggregator:	http://drupal.org/project/javascript_aggregator
Memcache:	http://drupal.org/memcache
Path Cache:	http://drupal.org/project/pathcache
Term lower name:	http://drupal.org/project/lowername
Varnish:	http://drupal.org/project/varnish

11.3   Analyzing

Some analytical functionality is provided in the Report section of your Drupal site with the Syslog and Statistics modules installed and enabled. These functionalities are quite basic and in some cases put extra load on the database, and thus may end up inimical to performance enhancement. There are third-party analytic platforms however, which would take much of the hard work out of the hands of the Drupal core and can also be easily integrated into Drupal by the addition of a bit of code embedded in a module. The following are the most popular of these analytics modules.

11.3.1   Google Analytics

http://drupal.org/project/google_analytics

Google Analytics is perhaps the most popular web analytics solution that presently exists. It assists you to see and analyze your traffic data for such purposes as improving marketing effectiveness and optimizing content.

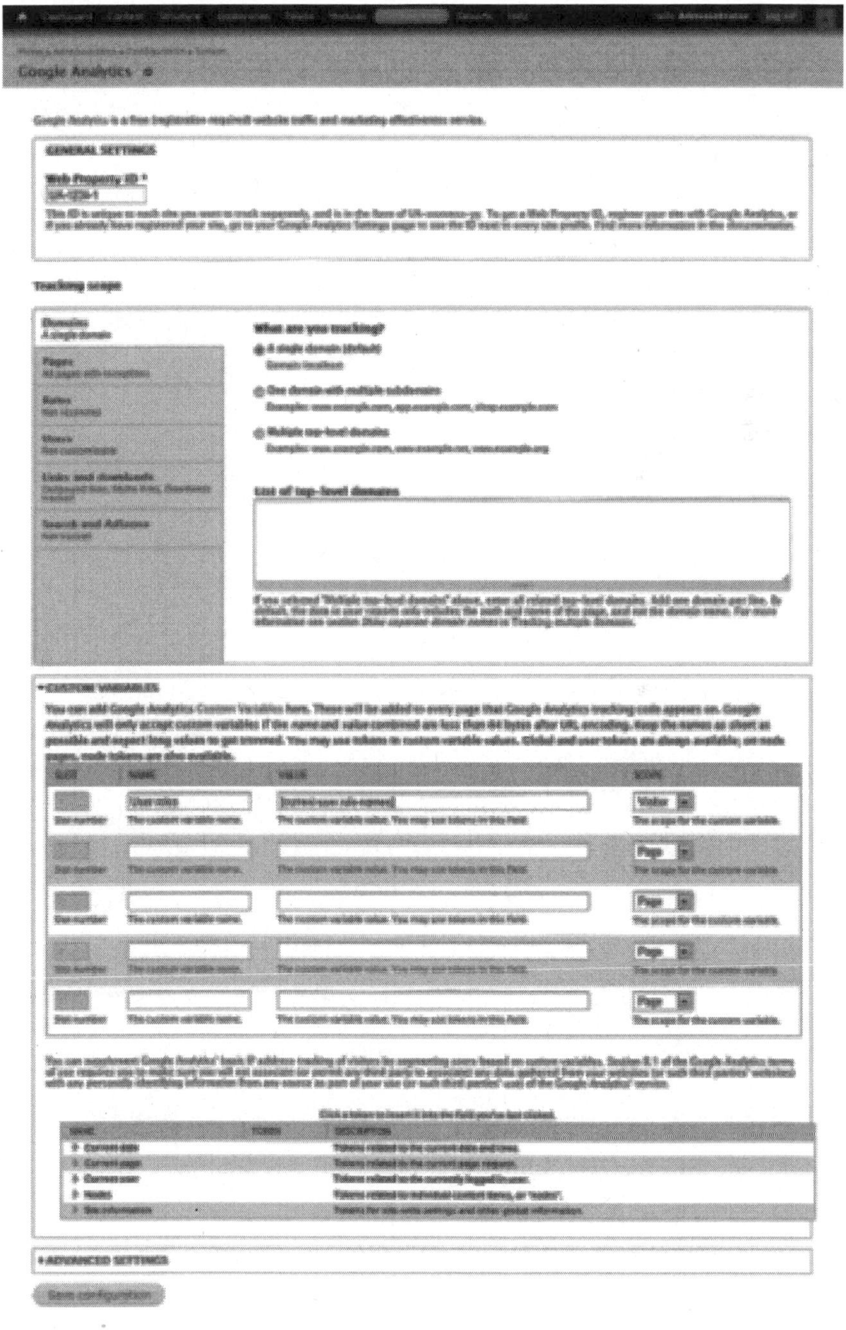

Figure 11.9   Google analytics module configuration page

Contributed Google Analytics modules can be added to your Drupal site which provides the following statistical features:

- Single/multi/cross domain tracking
- Selectively track/exclude certain users, roles and pages
- Monitor what type of links are tracked (downloads, outgoing and mailto)
- Monitor what files are downloaded from your pages
- Custom variables support with tokens
- Custom code snippets
- Site search support
- AdSense support
- Tracking of goals
- Anonymize visitor IP addresses
- Cache the Google Analytics code on your local server for improved page loading times
- Access denied (403) and Page not found (404) tracking
- DoNotTrack support (non-cached content only)

11.3.2   Yahoo! Web Analytics

http://drupal.org/project/yahoo_web_analytics

Yahoo! Web Analytics stores data in raw, non-aggregated form, and is more than simply a reporting tool. It is also a powerful, and highly flexible, data analysis tool able to instantly segment and visualize near real-time and historical data, with advanced graphs. The objective is to help marketers and site designers increase sales and visitor satisfaction, reduce marketing costs, and gain new insight on online customers.

The contributed Yahoo! Web Analytics module adds tracking functionality to a Drupal site, and allows administrators to do the following:

- Selectively track pages
- Map specific session variables to Yahoo! Web Analytics custom session fields
- Track Yahoo! Web Analytics actions, custom page view fields, and document fields on specific site paths
- Track site search keywords and result counts
- Track subdomain links as internal or external/exit links

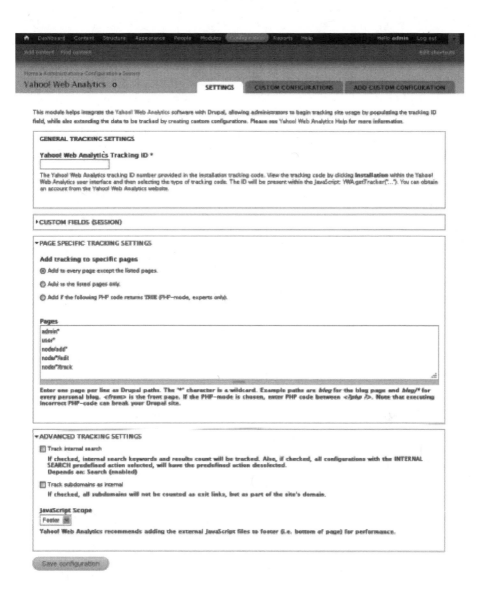

Figure 11.10   Yahoo web analytics module configuration page

11.3.3   Piwik Web analytics

http://www.drupal.org/project/piwik

Piwik aims to be an open source alternative to Google Analytics. It is a downloadable, open source real time web analytics software program which may be self-hosted or subscribed to on a software as a service basis (such as Google Analytics and Yahoo! Analytics). The main advantage of self-hosted Piwik and software as a service is that with Piwik, all visitor interaction data stays under control and ownership of the webmaster or company. Like other popular services, Piwik can check out who has been visiting your page, how, when, and why. This should enable you create goals and track conversions.

Figure 11.11   Piwik web analytics module configuration page

There is a Piwik module available for Dupal and it enables you add the following statistics features to your site:

- Single/multi domain tracking

- Selectively track/exclude certain users, roles and pages
- Monitor what files are downloaded from your pages
- Cache the Piwik code on your local server for improved page loading times
- Custom variables support with tokens
- Custom code snippets
- Site search plugin support
- Access denied (403) and Page not found (404) tracking
- DoNotTrack support

Figure 11.12   Piwik reporting page

11.4   Summary

The purpose of this chapter has been to show how to improve the performance of a Drupal website both for the benefit of users' as well as other stakeholders. This can be affected by following good practice suggestions which will help to effectively monitor, optimize and analyze the performance of the live site, to good advantage.

The chapter also provides suggestions on required and optional core features. It advises on where to get additional tools for performance enhancement, primarily by means of contributed modules as well as third party monitoring, optimization and analysis services.

Index